THE ENTREPRENEUR'S

GUIDE

TO BUSINESS BASICS

101

THE ENTREPRENEUR'S

GUIDE

TO BUSINESS BASICS

101

by

Jo Ann M. Colton

ISBN: 1-58721-961-1

Edited by: Bonni G. Spivak

The Write Approach, Las Vegas, NV

1st Books Rev. 11/7/00

ABOUT THE BOOK

If you are at the crossroads of your career and wondering which direction will lead you to the high road toward personal and professional success…*this book is for you*. If you already know which route you want to take, but you just need some words of encouragement and motivation to guide you on your life's journey…*this book is for you*. If you've dreamt about the independence and financial rewards of being your own boss, but don't know which path to follow or how to make your dreams come true…*this book is for you*.

The Entrepreneur's Guide to Business Basics 101 gives you a step-by-step overview of the requirements and responsibilities of business ownership. Learn how to choose the specific business just right for you. Discover how your business success may actually depend on choosing the right name for your business. From business sites to working with governmental agencies, from marketing and advertising to the human resources connection, you'll soon realize there's more to starting a business than merely obtaining your business license. Not everyone is cut out to be an entrepreneur. This book invites you to explore all the possibilities and investigate all the opportunities available to you. Find out if *you* have what it takes to start your own business.

The Entrepreneur's Guide to Business Basics 101 also follows an *A-B-C* ("**a**bsolutely-**b**asic-**c**an-do") approach to success with an alphabet of motivational messages to assist you in evaluating and setting goals and achieving them through self-realization. Why keep asking yourself questions, when you could be finding the answers you need? The key to success is through *"awareness"*. Become enlightened and travel the expressway toward self-discovery and self-improvement. No matter which career path you choose to follow, **The Entrepreneur's Guide to Business Basics 101** can help *you* be the best *you* can be!

ACKNOWLEDGEMENT

I would like to thank my friend Bonni Spivak not only for her editing of this book, but for her encouragement and support.

To *Bobo*...

This one's for you!

INTRODUCTION

Many people dream of being their own boss and owning their own business. Unfortunately, for many the dream stops there and the reality remains...just a dream. Often the reason for this is simply the lack of direction--not knowing *what* to do, *where* to begin or exactly *how* to make that dream come true. Though there are some among you that may think there is a secret to making the dream come true—there is no secret. The purpose of this book is to help readers help themselves. There's a lot of truth in that old saying, "nothing ventured, nothing gained". Only you alone can determine if owning your own business would be the right career path to follow. Only you hold the key to unlocking the entrepreneurial skills within you. For those who are willing to take an objective look at the possibilities of self-employment, finding the answers is as easy as ..... *"A-B-C"*.

The information contained herein is offered as a *general* guide based on my personal experiences as an entrepreneur and business owner of two liquor store/junior markets, a clothing partnership; and a promotional writing service for corporate, business and individual clients. The text boxes appearing in various chapters denote <u>specific</u> information relating to my experience with procedures I've followed or things I've encountered in my own business operations.

My administrative skills and supervisory/management experience have served me well to ensure my success as a business owner. I have called upon the sum of all my skills and knowledge as a realtor, office manager and human resources professional and have woven them into the foundation upon which this book is written. My background as a writer has provided the threads of continuity necessary to complete the final summation of information contained upon these pages.

How easy it would have been for my husband and me years ago, if there were then a business guidebook to follow. However, that part of our "dream" was never realized. But, the other part of the dream my husband and I shared, of owning our own business, we made that dream a reality for ourselves. As the author of <u>The Entrepreneur's</u>

<u>Guide to Business Basics 101</u>, it is my hope that my book will help you turn your own dream into reality for you.

This book is presented to its readers as "information only" from my personal perspective and experiences as a supervisor, manager and human resources professional in the corporate world; as an entrepreneur and business co-owner of two liquor store/junior markets; as a co-owner of a clothing partnership and as an owner of a corporate, business and personal promotional writing service.

Be aware that laws relating to businesses and human resources are constantly changing. The intention of this book is only to provide <u>awareness</u> and <u>motivation</u> to its readers so that readers can make their own life choices.

This book is not intended to render, or be a substitute for, legal advice; nor does it make any expressed or implied guarantees regarding the use of the information contained herein.

If you have specific questions about starting a business in your area, address them to the proper state and local governmental agencies in your city or county. Questions relating to legal issues involving your business and/or hiring practices should be directed to a legal professional licensed in your state.

TABLE OF CONTENTS

"A" is for: AWARENESS

Knowledge is derived from the study or investigation of a particular subject. With knowledge comes the assurance and confidence in one's ability. That feeling of confidence is the force that enables us to weigh options, define our choice of action and ultimately make decisions. Think "AWARENESS" for it can lead you to your destiny and provide you with:

Access to the information you need to understand "How to Start Your Own Business"

Ways to enable you to "weigh" your options

Ability to assess all available business opportunities

Resources to assist you in your quest

Enlightenment to unleash your entrepreneurial spirit

Need...the hunger to succeed

Empowerment to enter the new millennium as your *own* boss

Skills to help you achieve your vision

Satisfaction

📁CHAPTER I

TAKING THE FIRST STEP

Congratulations on purchasing this book! You are now one step closer to making a life-altering decision regarding whether or not you should open up a business and become your own boss. It is a difficult decision to make and one that should be contemplated carefully over a period of time before making up your mind. There are so many things to consider about business ownership. Each factor must be analyzed carefully to help ensure that you will be successful in your new endeavor. Don't set yourself up for failure by not thinking things through in a methodical manner. Take your time and consider all business options available to you. Get the facts, research all possibilities and consider the pros and cons of each.

Are you sure you're up to facing the challenges of self-employment and working through the trials and tribulations of becoming a business owner? If your answer is "yes", with a little bit of perseverance and a lot of determination you *can* make that career change and travel the entrepreneurial road to independence and financial success. Deciding to *open* your business is the easy part, deciding *what* business to open can be a bit more difficult.

It's nothing to worry about. You are one step closer to redirecting your career path and redefining your future, but you still have a lot of things to work out before applying for that business license. Are you wondering what's next? See for yourself; turn the page.

"B" is *for*: BELIEFS

Your *beliefs* comprise your understanding and acceptance of life's truths as you interpret them. Consequently, your personal beliefs will constitute the very foundation upon which your business operation will be built. Your opinions and convictions about how you will do business with your public and how you view customer service and the importance of serving your customer will be mirrored in your own principles of ethics, your own morals system and the rules of conduct to which you personally subscribe. This "way of doing business" is identified as your business culture. Your business culture is one that your customers will recognize and identify with your company. Be sure the business culture your customers see mirrors your own vision of your beliefs and business philosophy.

NOTES:

☐ CHAPTER II

EXPLORING BUSINESS
OPPORTUNITIES

Now that you are seriously considering self-employment, the next step is to determine what type of business would be right for you. Yet, before you can really decide you'll have to prioritize your needs and expectations of business ownership. Ask yourself the following questions:

1. Am I looking for full-time income or just a part-time business outlet?
2. Do I want to work the business alone?
3. Do I want the responsibility of maintaining employees?
4. No matter which direction I follow, how do I plan to raise start-up capital?

5. What are the advantages, disadvantages and expenses of operating a home-based business?

6. What are the advantages, disadvantages and expenses of operating a business requiring rented space?

The way you answer the first three questions will have a direct bearing on your course of action in researching and finding the answers to the last three questions.

Types of Business Ownership

Sole Proprietorship - The exclusive ownership of a business by only one individual.

Partnership - A voluntary association between two or more persons to participate in a business or venture under specific terms which are defined and mutually agreed upon as to participation, profit and losses.

Corporation - Consisting of a group of persons, a corporation is established and treated as an individual with rights and liabilities distinct and apart from those of the persons involved therein. A corporation has certain powers and duties of a natural person and under state corporation laws, a corporation may continue to exist for any length of time as prescribed by law.

"C" *is for*: CHANGE

Nothing in life stays the same. How many times have we heard someone state that to us? Even though our lives may seem to be constant and our routines and schedules may appear to be the same each day, things are <u>not</u> always what they seem. Whether or not we want to admit it, there is probably a lot of truth in that saying. Oh, there are probably some among you who have doubts; but the truth is that the only constant in life is *change*.

Although change is considered to be anything that transforms or replaces that which is familiar, change is all around us. Every day of our lives minor alterations of nature and life take place: the cost of living can fluctuate, peoples' moods can differ, climate and weather conditions can vary, one gray hair appears, gasoline prices increase, the scale indicates another pound gained. Many "changes" are often so subtle that they are rarely acknowledged; consequently, they are treated as the status quo. However, the passing of time usually has a way of making us take a retrospective look at our lives. It is most likely, if not inevitable, that at some point in our recollection and reflection of our life's accomplishments and memories we will come face to face with the realization that change *has* occurred.

Most people do not accept change very well. As creatures of habit, we find security in that which is constant and familiar. Change invades our feelings of well being and can even invoke hysterical fear in some people. Quite possibly it is the uncertainty of the unknown that causes some people to view change with such resistance.

Because everything in life has a positive and a negative side, change, too, can be positive as well as negative. If everything always stayed the same, life could get very boring. Change can be the catalyst for opportunity…as in the opportunity to regroup our thoughts and restructure the direction of our lives. Change can transform our looks, energize our self-esteem and even carry us from a dead-end job to an exciting business opportunity of self-employment. Maybe it's time to change our minds about *change...*

🗁 CHAPTER III

HOME BASED BUSINESSES

A home-based business has a lot of advantages with the obvious ones being that you won't have to leave your house, you can make your own hours and you will not have to answer to anyone except yourself. It does sound good, but like anything else in life there are positive and negative aspects to consider. Will it work for you? Only you can make that judgment. First, "go with what you know"...

Making Assessments

Do you have a life-long hobby that can be expanded into a viable business? For instance, a tropical fish hobbyist may decide he or she has enough knowledge and know-how to open up a home service business that will focus on setting up and cleaning fish tank aquariums for its individual or business clients. Or, maybe you are an expert at sewing. If so, consider becoming a full-time seamstress specializing is doing alterations from your home. Take stock of all your skills and experience and capitalize on them. If you're an excellent typist, why not start a typing service? Do you love working outdoors in your garden? A landscaping service may be in your future. Are you a walking botanical encyclopedia? Your expert knowledge of plants may make you a sought after speaker with "how to grow..." plant enthusiasts.

As you explore your options, you will also have to study the feasibility of each. Ask yourself:

1. Is there a need for this type of business in my area?
2. Who are my customers and how will I reach them?
3. Can I run this type of business alone or will I need employees?
4. Do I want (or need) a partner?
5. What type of equipment and supplies are necessary for this operation?

Finding Answers to Your Questions

1. *Is there a need for this type of business in my area?* Refer to the yellow pages of your local telephone book and search for listings or display ads for comparable businesses in your community. Peruse your local newspaper to see if the goods and/or services of similar businesses are being advertised therein. If you cannot find businesses in the

field of your pursuit, it may mean there is little need or market to support such a venture. Should this prove to be true, come up with other business ideas until you find one that will work for you.

2. *Who are my customers and how will I reach them?* When you come up with a business idea that seems feasible to you, make a list of the groups of people who would benefit the most from the products or services you want to offer.

3. *Can I run this type of business alone or will I need employees?* Before you can conclusively answer this question you will have to make some decisions about the type of business you will pursue.

4. *What are the advantages or disadvantages of having a partner?* Again, the answer to this question has many components based on type of business, the amount and availability of start-up capital, business location and income potential.

5. *What types of equipment and supplies are necessary for this operation?* The answer to this question will be clearly evident once you decide on the specific business of your choice.

Examples of Home-Based Businesses

The ideas and opportunities for home-based businesses are virtually endless and are only limited by one's own creativity and imagination. To help you consider the possibilities, I've listed some that you may want to pursue.

1. Arts & Crafts (selling your own work or the work of others on consignment)
2. Automobile Detailer (mobile business where you go to your customer's location)
3. Business Consultant
4. Carpet Cleaning
5. Child Care
6. Fitness Trainer
7. House Cleaning
8. House Fix-it & Repair Service (small repairs)
9. House Painting
10. House/Pet Sitting
11. Music Lessons (guitar, piano, voice. . .)
12. Medical Billing Processor
13. Medical Claims Processor
14. Medical Transcriber
15. Personal Shopper
16. Photographer (free-lance)

17. Pool Cleaning

18. Wall Paper Hanging

19. Window Cleaning

20. Writer - Promotional

21. Writer - Resumes

As you continue to explore the possibility of starting a home-based business, one fact will become very obvious to you: not every type of business can be operated from home. Your research will reveal that the logistics involved in some types of businesses just do not lend themselves to a residential environment. In addition, most cities have strict health and zoning guidelines governing the types of businesses that can be operated from a residence. Be sure to contact your hometown's licensing entities and inquire about zoning, health and environmental regulations in your neighborhood.

To Work at Home or Not Work at Home...That is the Question

If you are one of the many people who choose to start a home-based business, I commend you. Such an endeavor is not for everyone. If you work better with, and among others, this situation may not be ideal for you. On the other hand, if you are a self-starter who loves the thrill of a challenge, you will surely enjoy this environment.

Clearly, the best part of owning a home-based business is being able to stay home and create flexible working hours. This unstructured work environment "works" well for the person who is not only dedicated, but highly motivated as well.

Beware! You must possess a strong desire to succeed and be able to operate within the parameter of "structured" flexibility. By this I mean that you should set your business guidelines and work within them. Once your friends and relatives are aware that you have opted to work at home, they will probably feel that your being home gives them the relaxed opportunity to call you during the day just to "chat" and pass time. Staying focused is very important to your business and financial success. To be successful, stringent time management skills must be followed to maximize output and eliminate non-productivity. Therefore, it is up to you to set *your* business rules and remind all concerned that you are working.

Before you move forward, make sure that you have clearly identified your product or service. Establish not only who your targeted customer market will be, but also how you will go about reaching them. Businesses located in strip malls, shopping centers, business parks or industrial areas enjoy the visibility of being noticed day after day as people drive or walk past the building. However, because a home-based operation does not have any visibility to the outside world, you must be willing and able to employ all the advertising and marketing techniques available to you to create your own visibility. (Refer to Chapter 12 – Marketing and Chapter 13 – Advertising).

Business Furniture & Equipment

Most home-based business will start out with the basics:

1. Computer and Printer
2. Desk
3. Desk/Computer Chair
4. Telephone
5. Telephone Answering Machine
6. Fax Machine
7. Filing Cabinet
8. Office supplies (pens, pencils, stapler, stapler remover, scotch tape, typing paper, scratch pads, telephone message pads, hanging folders, file folders)

Some businesses may require a copy machine. Will this be necessary for your particular business? Now that you have the basics, you must consider your needs based upon your specific business. If you are creating gift baskets from your home you will need special supplies related to that business: baskets, basket filler, cellophane wrapping, ribbons, bows, decorations, basket items (candies, stuffed animals...or whatever you plan to offer in your baskets). If you are starting a pool service you will need pool-cleaning equipment, chemicals to test the acid and chlorine levels of the water, and so on...

Capital

A certain amount of money will be necessary to start your business. This investment is called *start-up* money. To figure out how much money you will need to open your business you will have to firmly decide what type of business you will open. Once this determination has been made, you will need to attach a monetary value to the following items to determine how much start-up money will be required.

1. Business licenses and/or related fees
2. Fictitious Firm Name Filing Fees

3. Insurance bonds, health certificates etc. (Contact your local governing agencies for business licenses and zoning to find out if such bonds and fees apply to your business.)

4. Basic business equipment (and specialty equipment, if applicable).

5. Installation fees for phone and fax lines (if applicable).

6. Office supplies

7. Office furniture (desk, chairs, work table)

8. Enough working capital to keep your business "in business" for at least the next six months. To determine this you must figure what your monthly recurring expenses will be.

9. If your product is taxable, you will be required to get a state sales tax certificate.

Recurring Expenses

Your monthly recurring expenses represent monies you know you will have to pay out either on a monthly, quarterly or yearly basis. Monthly expenses can include telephone bill, sales tax, advertising, supplies, membership fees (Chamber of Commerce, specific organizations relating to your business . . .), business magazine subscriptions, contracted labor or consultant fees (services of a typist, desk-top publisher, etc.), raw materials relating to your product or service. Quarterly expenses may encompass sales tax payments (sales tax may be monthly, quarterly or yearly depending on the laws of the state in which you live) and other business related fees. Yearly expenses would be income tax, state tax (if applicable), business license renewals. List all your recurring monthly expenses and total them up. Now multiply the figure by 6 months (or if you think it will take longer to gain momentum in your home-based business, multiply the figure by 12). The grand total should be entered as #8 on your "Start-Up Money Needed" list.

"D" *is for*: DETERMINATION

Determination is the unfaltering intent of purpose directed at attaining a specific goal. Fueled by high-octane energy and the driving force to succeed, determination is the vehicle that will carry you to your desired destination.

NOTES:

□CHAPTER 4

BUSINESS SITES
(RETAIL/OFFICE/INDUSTRIAL
SPACE)

Business brokers and commercial real estate agents will tell you that when it comes to renting any kind of business space, there are only three important factors to consider:

1. Location! 2. Location! 3. Location! I remember this rule all too well from the real estate licensing training class I attended many years ago in California. I even remember learning that the shadiest side of the street (the south side) is considered the most desirable.

But, location means so much more than on which side of the street your business resides. The placement of the physical structure of your business has a direct bearing on the degree to which your business will be accessible and visible to your potential customers. Can your business sign be seen by cars that drive by? Is your storefront hidden from view by another store or adjacent building? If your business location is not visible to the public, it is highly unlikely that a potential customer would just "happen" upon your business. For all practical purposes; unless the public at large were able to "discover" your business in some other fashion, "out of sight", would equate to "out of mind"--which would result in "no sale".

From a safety standpoint, location is even more of a factor in some businesses than in others. For instance, while having an alleyway in close proximity to your clothing store may not affect your business operation with any significance, you may not want to operate your business near that same alley if your store were a liquor store and junior market.

In most cases there is a greater likelihood of robbery occurring at a liquor store than at a clothing store. If your type of business would be at greater risk than other types might be, you may want to pass on such a location, rather than provide a potential robber with an easy escape route via the alleyway.

Estimating the Cost of Rental Space

Rental costs will vary from city to city and state to state with some areas being slightly higher and some areas being slightly lower. The cost of rented space is based on a per foot value that can range from .75¢ per square foot to in excess of $1.50 per square foot. Again, rental location is a big factor in the price. Why? Because when it comes to renting any kind of business space, there are only three important factors to consider:

1. Location! 2. Location! 3. Location!

The more desirable the space in terms of accessibility and visibility to the prospective customers, the more money the landlord can command and will receive. The more amenities the space and the complex have to offer, the more you will pay to do business in that environment. Retail space is the most expensive. Office space is computed slightly lower than retail space; industrial space is the least expensive of the three.

If you were planning to open a retail business, your operation would not necessarily lend itself to an office space environment. The success of retail operations depends on a continuous flow of people coming in and out which makes store front space the best environment. Office space in most business complexes offers interior access, rather than street access, to each office unit. Because the "business" is not visible from the street it offers a lesser degree of accessibility and opportunity for revenue. It goes back to the "out of sight, out of mind" theory. In addition, many office space leases prohibit the degree of customer traffic that a retail business would necessitate. Reasons for this vary, but may include the additional risk of customer injury and owner-liability associated with the increased customer flow to the building, as well as the added noise disruption to the tenants whose business activity requires a more subdued working atmosphere. There are always exceptions to this rule. In the case of large downtown office buildings, the leasing offices may be willing to rent retail space to a restaurant or small business specializing in newspapers, cigarettes, packaged sandwiches, and snacks... These businesses would be marketed as a convenience to, and for, the other business tenants. The tenants and their employees would become the "ready-made" customers who would be more than willing to patronize these types of establishments. The location factor would definitely come into play here as the location itself would almost guarantee a "captive" clientele. Through mutually agreed upon lease negotiations these business opportunities have the potential of being lucrative, not only for the new storeowner, but advantageous to the building owner as well.

Don't overlook industrial parks, as they are not limited to warehouse businesses. Retail businesses are usually welcome and can thrive in such an environment. I have personally seen a variety of retail, service and office type businesses (printing shops, gift basket stores, flower shops, promotional writing services) successfully operate from industrial parks.

Look and Listen While You Shop Around

If you are seriously looking to buy an existing business, take your time to shop around. Don't make a hasty decision to buy the first place you see. When my husband and I first decided to go into business over twenty-five years ago, we took the time to weigh our options. The rule "go with what you know" also applies to large-scale businesses, not just home-based businesses.

My husband's family had owned a very successful market in downtown Los Angeles for many years. My husband had worked in the family business when he was a teenager. Years later he became a store manager of a well-known chain supermarket. If there was one thing my husband knew it was food and beverages (soda pop, beer, wine and alcohol).

The downside to this business opportunity for us was that we had a young and growing family and most liquor and junior market stores were open about 16 hours a day.

We needed some outside help to operate it and we didn't have a lot of money. After weighing the pros and cons of this type of business, estimating the cost of getting into this type of venture and evaluating our needs and our expectations, we decided this would be the "temporary" business for us. Temporary for us meant that we would keep the business for a specified number of years, make our money and then go on to something else. No matter what the future held, my husband had a trade and could always go back to that trade. The factor that weighed heavily in helping us make our decision was that my husband had a complete understanding of how to start and operate such a venture. In our minds this, above all, gave us an edge and we felt we could be successful. We were willing to give it a try, but we were not yet ready to rush into self-employment.

Instead, we looked...we listened...and we shopped around. We spent countless hours visiting every liquor store and junior market that was for sale in our community. My husband would take a stroll down each store aisle paying strict attention to the types of products in the store, how many cold display cases were available. With his trained eye, he would estimate the size of the walk-in box. Was it too small? Did the store have growth potential? I would pay attention to how well the store was stocked. Were the shelves stocked fully? Did the merchandise look like it turned over rapidly or did the products look old and worn out? Was the store clean? Would I feel comfortable shopping in it, if I were the customer? We would make mental notes of the pros and cons of each store we saw and would then write the information down on a pad as soon as we got into our car. Often we would sit in the parking lot for twenty or thirty minutes at a time to watch the customer flow of the operation. On our pad we would write down the number of customers coming in and out of the store in the time frame we were there. It was important to record whether the customers walked to the store and if so, where they walked from (nearby apartments, other businesses, or neighborhood housing tracts). If the customers drove to the store, we estimated the percentage of drive-in customers versus walk-in customers. Then we determined the size of the parking lot and factored in whether or not we felt the parking lot would adequately accommodate the proposed growth potential of the store. While we sat in the parking lot we also rated the outside of the establishment. Was the parking lot lighting adequate to ensure the safety of the customers? Was there an alleyway at the back of the parking lot? Alleys were out; we were not interested. We realized that when it came to the possibility of robbery, there were no guarantees. However, we wanted to eliminate all the adversity we felt we could control.

We were willing and eager to do our homework, including networking with other storeowners in the same type of business to get their opinions and input about each available business opportunity. The project was worth all the time and effort we put into it because the investment would be sizeable, which would make the thought of failure that much more devastating.

With me acting as Miss Marple to my husband's Hercule Poirot, we played detectives and shopped around in this manner for about one year. The more we saw, the more we developed a profile that told us what we wanted, what we definitely did not want and what we felt we could work with and improve upon. During this entire year we never approached the seller/storeowner. We visited each store as a "customer" and made our notes accordingly.

At last, when felt we were truly ready, we contacted a business broker specializing in liquor & junior markets. With his help we located the right business opportunity for us.

Leases: Retail/Office/Industrial

Whether you are a novice at business ownership or a seasoned entrepreneur, you may want to enlist the help of a business broker or commercial real estate agent to help you find the ideal location for your new business venture. As I've mentioned earlier, the three most important factors in starting any business are *location...location...location*! Business brokers and commercial real estate agents focus on the sale and/or lease of business opportunities, exclusively. Some agents even choose to specialize only in specific types of businesses (i.e. liquor stores, convenience stores etc.). The knowledge and experience they gain by specializing makes them experts in their chosen areas.

Many business owners thinking of selling their business will only deal with business brokers and agents and will not openly advertise to the public that their establishment is for sale. Consequently, should you decide to look around on your own, you may miss out on some of the better opportunities that are only available through the brokers' multiple listing service.

The fee of the business broker or agent is paid by the seller, not the buyer. The agent's services may prove helpful regardless of whether you are opening a new store in a soon-to-be-built strip mall or shopping center, or purchasing an existing business. Real estate professionals understand their business market, have access to a myriad of business opportunities in all areas of your city and are skilled in the art of lease negotiations.

Capital

Whether you operate your business from your home or from a rented business site, you will require start-up money to begin your operation. However, your monetary investment will likely be much more to begin your business from a rented storefront or office than from your home. Assess your start-up capital needs by reviewing the items below. The first seven items will apply to both a home-based business and a leased business site. The differences between the two business options become evident in items 8-15.

1. Business licenses and/or related fees

2. Fictitious Firm Name filing fees

3. *Insurance bonds, health certificates, etc. (Contact your local agencies governing business licenses and zoning laws business requirements to find out if such bonds, certificates and fees apply to your business.)

4. Basic business equipment (and specialty equipment, if applicable)

5. Installation fees for phone and fax lines (if applicable)

6. Office supplies

7. Office furniture (desk, chairs, work space table . . .)

8. Cash register (if yours is a retail operation)

9. Enough working capital to keep your business "in business" and sustain you in meeting your lease obligations and business expenses. Remember that the lease agreement is a contract. There are considerable legal consequences for defaulting on your lease in any manner.

10. Personal Liability Insurance

11. Insurance covering the interior of your store or office (inventory, merchandise and fixtures)

12. *Worker's Compensation Insurance (if you are hiring employees)

13. *State Unemployment Insurance (if you are hiring employees)

14. *State Sales Tax Certificate

15. Security Alarm System

*Note: *Bonds may be required for items #12-14*

Recurring Expenses

Recurring expenses represent monies you know you will have to pay out either on a monthly, quarterly or yearly basis. Monthly expenses can include rent, telephone bill, electricity, water, trash pick-up, advertising, supplies, membership fees (Chamber of Commerce, specific organizations relating to your business, Internet . . .), business magazine subscriptions, contracted labor or consultant fees, material vendors and suppliers. Based on your business's estimated gross monthly income and your state's laws, you may be instructed to pay state unemployment insurance, worker's compensation and state sales tax either monthly, quarterly or yearly. Yearly expenses would be income tax, state tax (if applicable), business license renewals.

List all your recurring expenses and total them up. Now multiply the total figure by 6 months or 12 months to determine your start-up capital.

NOTES:

"E" *is for*: EMPOWERMENT

If *power* can be defined as recognizing one's physical strength or acknowledging one's authority in expressed or implied situations, then the meaning of *"empower"* can be explained as enabling or giving permission to someone to perform or promote their ability to self-actualize a specific idea or goal. All things considered, it appears logical that *"empowerment"* must be the precursor to personal accomplishment.

Many people feel unable to act in any capacity that requires initiative for reasons that usually involve lack of direction, lack of knowledge or a lack of authority. Excuses for non-performance often include such reasons as: "I'm waiting for a better job opportunity to come along"; I'm waiting until next year, then I'll start thinking of making a change"; or "I'm waiting for my ship to come in" . . . Wait too long and opportunity will pass you by. Procrastinate too often and you'll discover the ship you were waiting for has sunk! *Empower* yourself! You don't need permission from anyone to take charge of your own life.

It is a matter of individual choice whether or not to allow ourselves to unleash our own power. To choose to do so is to choose the opportunity to embark on an exciting journey into self-realization. Such an experience can help us discover that we can help to direct our own destiny. We have the power to create a whole New World for ourselves where career opportunities abound through optimistic eyes and personal self-fulfillment is ours to seek out and enjoy. However, should we choose to suppress our own potential by not taking action, then we each render ourselves powerless.

In this game of life there are two types of people: those who wait for things to happen and those who make things happen. Which one are you? Remember that power comes from within...*empower* yourself and find the answer.

📂CHAPTER 5

LEASES

We will be discussing leases from the point of view of leasing a *business opportunity* located in retail, office or industrial space. A *business opportunity* involves the sale of personal (chattel) property, including the sale of inventory, fixtures, goodwill and the assignment of a lease or license. *Inventory* defines a complete list of stock being transferred. Inventory is not included in a bill of sale and is figured separate and apart from any items that may be included in a bill of sale. *Fixtures,* in this sense, refer to any items attached by a tenant for use in his trade or the operation of his business. (Fixtures in a liquor store may include the merchandise shelves, walk-in box, frozen food cases, ice machine . . .) *Goodwill* represents the expectation of continued patronage of the business's current customer base.

A *lease* is a contract between an owner (lessor) and a tenant (lessee) setting forth a specified term for which the tenant may occupy the real property, as well as the conditions relating to the tenant's use of the designated property. (A lease may also be written with a purchase option clause in which the lessee, the person leasing the property, may reserve the right to purchase the real property should it be offered for sale by the owner at a later date.) Like all contracts, a lease must be based upon consideration (in this situation it would be the rent paid by the lessee).

There is no standardized language required in a lease. However, the lease must contain: the names of the parties involved, description of the property being leased, the dollar amount of the rent to be paid (and due dates of the rent), the period of time for which the lease will begin and end, and the signatures of the parties.

When entering into lease negotiations, plan not only for the present time, but also for your business's future. For example, don't just set your sights on securing a 5 year lease; be sure to include a lease option clause that gives you the right to renew the lease (at your discretion) for another designated time period (i.e. an additional 5 or 10 years). Likewise, you will want the lease to allow you the right to assign, at your option, your leasehold rights to another buyer and sell your license(s), if a special license is required to operate your business operation (i.e. a liquor license). Having such options in your lease gives you leverage in the event that at some future time you want to sell your business. A prospective buyer will not want to buy a business that guarantees him only one or two remaining years of your original leasehold interest, without some type of guarantee that the landlord will choose to rewrite the lease at the end of its term. Entering into such a business venture is risky for your buyer and could cost him a lot of money in legal and/or relocation costs if the landlord opts not to rewrite for him the same type of lease you originally negotiated.

I reiterate that a lease is a contract. Before entering into, and signing, any lease agreement make sure you understand the type and terms of the lease the lessor is offering you. The following list represents types of "term" leases.

1. <u>Flat, Fixed or Straight Lease </u> - This lease is for a fixed period of time at a set rate of rent.

2. <u>Graduated Lease</u> - This lease provides for a varying rental rate, often based on future determination (i.e. based

on your business's projected revenue increases on a monthly basis).

3. <u>Net Lease</u> - This lease is based on the tenant paying a portion of the entire lessor's (landlord's) operating expenses (taxes, insurance, etc.) giving the lessor (landlord/owner) a net amount of income.

4. <u>Percentage Lease</u> - A lease in which the rental amount is based on the amount of business done by the lessee (tenant); usually a percentage of gross receipts. The higher the gross receipts, the lower the rate.

If you are serious about purchasing an existing business, become familiar with the business terms listed below. At an early point in your purchase negotiations you will want to have the owner show you the business's accounting books (accounts receivable/accounts payable), the last three years of tax returns for the business and all documentation as noted in items #1-5.

1. **Balance Sheet** - A statement of the business's financial position at any given time, listing assets, liabilities and net worth.

2. **Assets** – The economic resources of a company (what is owned). Assets include:

a.   Cash and securities

b.   Accounts receivable

c.   Stocks in trade - inventory

d.   Real estate (if applicable) and equipment

e.   Prepaid insurance, rents or taxes

f.   Goodwill

3. **Liabilities** - A creditor's claims, or what is owed. Liabilities include:

a.   Accounts or notes payable

b.   Accrued wages, salaries or commissions

c.   Interest due on loans

d.   Unpaid taxes

4. **Net Worth** - Represents the owner's equity or the difference between assets and liabilities.

An equation to remember is:

Net Worth = (A-L) Assets <u>minus</u> Liabilities

Assets = (L+NW) Liabilities <u>plus</u> Net Worth

Liabilities = (A-NW) Assets <u>minus</u> Net Worth

5. **Profit and Loss Statement** - Shows the revenues, expenses and net income (or loss) for a given period of time.

A business broker or commercial real estate agent engaged in the sale of a *business opportunity* must have a basic understanding of financial statements in order to analyze a prospective business for his client. Again, this is another reason to consider engaging the service of a *business opportunity* professional.

"F" *is for*: FUTURE

We never get to live our future because
it moves ever quickly to become our past.
The future hovers just beyond our daydreams...
An illusion that was never meant to last.

Often described as a vision of time and things to come, the future is as elusive as a butterfly. People are always speaking about the future and dreaming of what lies ahead. The promise of the future manifests itself to us in many ways...as in the smile of someone we adore, in the look of a wide-eyed child, in the soft, breathy whisper of a warm summer's breeze or in the loud, thunderous roar of the heavens on a stormy night.

We have often heard talk of the future with words like "the future looks bright ahead"; "look to the future and you will find your answers"; "you have your whole future ahead of you". Some people envision the brass ring of life dangling just inches beyond their reach and wonder why their future eludes them. The truth of the matter is that the future is only a state of mind—it is our perception of how we each envision the subsequent remainder of our lives.

Life can be divided into three units of measure: yesterday, today and tomorrow. Our *yesterday* encompasses the many pieces of time we've experienced in our lives. With each passing day we add another "yesterday" to our pile. Stored securely in our mind's memory box, these times and events belong to our *past*. We miss them. Ah, yes; but we have the glorious promise of each new tomorrow to ease our sorrow. *Tomorrow* speaks of the moments of times in our lives yet to come. Tomorrow is our *future...* representing the portion of our lives that lay ahead—our hopes and our dreams for our good health, happiness, love and success in days and years to come. Dreams are wonderful and fanciful, but in our dreaming of the future let us not forget that the only real moments of time we have are in the present in which we reside. Make every minute of your life count...today! For *today*, is the only reality we have to ensure that our *future* will be all that we dream.

⌐CHAPTER 6

FRANCHISES

Franchise ownership is another type of business option available to you. A *franchise* represents permission given to a distributor or retailer (franchisee) from a manufacturer or corporation owner (franchiser) which gives entitlement to the franchisee to sell the owner's products.

Representing an array of products and services from coffee drinks to convenience stores, from fast-food chains to full-service restaurants . . . there are a variety of franchise businesses to consider. Start-up costs for franchise businesses will vary depending on: type of business, the equipment necessary to operate the leasehold improvements and of course, location. Typically, a breakdown of start-up items to consider might represent the following:

1. Franchise Purchase Fee

This could be as little as $10,000 or in excess of $50,000. The cost of the franchise depends on the type of franchise you purchase and the location.

2. Opening Inventory

The cost of this depends on the type of product you'll be offering, its base cost and the start-up quantity necessary.

3. Equipment, Fixtures, Signage, & Leasehold Improvements

Depending on the magnitude of your operation, this cost could be well in excess of $100,000.

4. Grand Opening Advertising

Estimate $10,000-$20,000 for this item.

5. Rent & Security Deposit

Usually one month's rent, plus specified security deposit.

6. Training Expenses

The franchiser will offer training instruction on how to operate your business, prepare the product (in the case of food or drink), maintain equipment etc. As the cost of this training will vary from franchiser to franchiser, $3,000-$5000 would be an estimate of such an expense.

7. Miscellaneous Costs

Category for costs that do not fit into any other category. This may represent $3,000-$5,000.

8. Additional Funds

The franchiser may require an additional sum to hold in abeyance as a security cushion that will guarantee payment of your obligations for a specified period of time (perhaps 6 months) in the event your business does not build as quickly as anticipated. As an example: based on a monthly rent of $3,000 this would equate to $18,000.

9. Ongoing Costs

As a franchisee, you will be required to pay a percentage rate usage fee for using the franchise name, a national marketing fee and, if applicable, a fee to maintain membership in a local group of the company's franchise owners.

The Internet can help you find out more about franchise businesses. Surf the web and explore the many web sites available to you. Once you find a franchise opportunity you want to pursue contact the company's franchise development department. They will have you fill out a candidate profile package. The company's receipt of your completed package will initiate negotiations. The franchise department will help you determine whether or not franchise ownership would be right for you. If there's a two-way match, they will work toward developing your franchise concept and location.

"G" *is for*: GOALS

The best way to get something done is to do it! Maybe you are saying to yourself, "sounds easy, but how do I get started?" My answer to you would be "one step at a time, of course."

The first thing you must consider is what you want to accomplish. The results or achievements toward which your efforts are directed are considered to be your *"goals"*. It is important to set goals that are realistic as well as attainable. Once you have defined your goals you must decide what steps you must take in order to achieve them.

The actions taken toward realizing your goals are your *"objectives"*. Be sure to allow a reasonable time frame in which you expect to complete each task on your list. Although we may all want to get things done as quickly as possible, the quick approach is not always the most feasible or the most effective way of getting the job completed.

Likewise, it may fall short of the end result you are anticipating.

It is important to think things out carefully, even if it means proceeding just a little more slowly than originally anticipated. Take your time, plan ahead, and get organized. Writing your goals and objectives on paper enables you to analyze all your information and provides you with a broader, more visual overview of the entire project. Think of accomplishing your goals, as you would think of walking down the street or climbing a flight of stairs... It's definitely easier if you do it "one step at a time".

🗀 CHAPTER 7

BUSINESS FURNITURE/FIXTURES /EQUIPMENT

Home-based businesses and offsite business locations do share a need for the following: desk, computer, printer, business telephone, fax machine, file cabinets, pens, pencils, paper, desk supplies . . .In addition, retailers will need a cash register. The type of business furniture, fixtures and/or equipment required to open a retail store, office, service or industrial-based business will vary greatly depending on the type of business, the type of space, and your targeted customer market.

Much of the needed office furniture and basic office equipment (including copier machines) can be purchased reasonably through discount membership stores. Specialty equipment can be costly so you might have to do some checking around to get the best prices. Trade papers and newspaper classified ads may alert you to similar businesses like your own that may be going out of business and are willing to sell off their fixtures and equipment at discounted rates.

Take a realistic approach to your business needs. While business image is important, don't make high-end purchases that you really cannot afford. Depending on your business, start-up costs can be steep enough without compounding such costs. Be aware of your spending limitations. You can purchase nice looking business furniture and convey the business image you want to convey, while staying within the budget you know you can afford.

When purchasing business equipment, assess your company's requirements. Even if you could afford the most expense equipment, it may not suit your business needs. Once you determine the equipment and features you feel are important to your operation then estimate the projected frequency of use for each piece of equipment. Be sure to factor in service repair and maintenance fees. In the long run you may be better off if your initial equipment investments are made somewhere in the middle-range of the available product lines. However, this is a decision only you can make. Review all the information you've gathered to help you make the most cost-effective decision regarding your equipment purchases. As your business operation becomes financially successful you can "upgrade" your furniture and/or equipment on an "as-needed" basis.

NOTES:

"H" *is for*: HABITS

Whether we realize it or not, habits are a part of our daily lives. We all do certain things as a matter of habit as: *reaching for the salt or pepper shaker before we've even tasted our food, laughing to cover up feelings of insecurity or nervousness, repeatedly twirling strands of our hair as we talk, not making eye contact when we speak to another due to the insecurity of the moment or the lack of confidence in ourselves...*

Habits are specific actions that are done over and over again until they become second nature in that they require no conscious thoughts to performing them. Some habits are "good" because they produce positive results (i.e. the habit of being punctual; the habit of getting the required amount of sleep, the habit of meeting defined work deadlines, the habit of paying your bills on time. . .). Other types of habits may be "bad", producing negative and even harmful results. When a habit is taken to excess it becomes an addiction (i.e. drug, alcohol, food or gambling addictions).

Because habits are *unconscious* actions and are difficult to change, change can only be made when a <u>*conscious*</u> effort is made to do so. Changing a habit requires the willingness and desire for change, a focused mind-set and the use and support of positive reinforcement towards the change.

Do you have any habits you would like to change? If so, now is the time to do it! Don't procrastinate any longer. Be the captain of your own ship and chart your own course in life. If you decide that self-employment is for you, you can opt to be the owner of your own company and find the success for which you have dreamed. Remember that habits are hard to break and taking control of yourself is a good habit to form because it will produce positive results for you. "Get in the habit" of taking a pro-active, rather than a reactive, approach to your life...and your career.

NOTES:

🗀CHAPTER 8

START-UP MONIES/BUSINESS PLAN

Identifying Sources for Start-Up Capital

Funding is an important consideration in starting any business and it is something to be concerned with early in your assessment of whether or not to start a business. Not only must you determine from where you will secure start-up money, but also how easy (or difficult) it will be to pay it back under the specified terms of the loan.

First, assess what resources may be available to you and then compare and contrast each option. Start with the bank that handles your personal accounts and see what they have to offer. The Small Business Administration (SBA) is another source to be recognized. You can quickly find out about SBA loans by searching on the Internet. The information provided would indicate various banks that make small business loans. Additional data can be learned from the booklets: **SBA Borrower's Guide** and **SBA**

Programs & Services, which are available to you free of charge through the U.S. General Services Administration. The material discusses SBA's loan programs and explains how SBA can assist you in your business start-up plans as well as business expansion projects. You can visit the Consumer Information Center web site at: www.pueblo.gsa.gov to view the full text of these booklets or to order printed copies.

Loans can also be secured from family and/or friends, but I urge you to proceed with caution in this area. Loans of this nature are often not treated as "business transactions" by the parties involved due to their family ties or close personal relationships. As a result, "misunderstandings" arise over the terms and repayment of the monies. In some cases, the loan never gets repaid causing a strain on the family relationship or dissolution of the friendship. If you choose to secure a loan from family and/or friends, be sure you write up an agreement which details the amount to be loaned, date of loan, terms of the loan, the amount of interest to be paid on the loan (if any) and any other pertinent information. If you must borrow from someone you know, my suggestion would be to ensure that all parties involved are of the same mindset as to whether or not the loan is a business or personal transaction. You may want to have the signatures of all parties involved in the loan notarized by a notary public.

Many years ago when my husband and I first went into business, we borrowed a fairly large sum of money from my in-laws. We drew up an agreement and stated the terms of the loan as indicated above. With both my husband and I being very independent and responsible people, we even opted to pay my in-laws ½ point over the current interest rate at that time for the monies we borrowed. Per the contract, every penny was paid back according to terms of that agreement. Treating the transaction as a business matter was the best thing we could have done as it eliminated any possibility of "lapses of memory", misinterpretations or misunderstandings by *"any"* of the parties involved—or by any other family members . . .

Depending on your type of business, grant monies may also be available to you. The library is a good beginning point of reference for identifying grant sources. Bookstores often carry books on the subject as well. Don't overlook local colleges or universities as they may offer classes on grant writing or be able to provide information on how to explore grant opportunities.

Creating A Business Plan

Whether or not you are trying to secure business capital, you must have a plan in order to prove (even to yourself) that your business is viable. While a written plan is an effective tool to you because putting it down on paper takes it from the conceptual state to the visual stage, a written business plan is essential for the lender to determine whether or not you will be given loan approval.

A business plan usually encompasses a 5-year span and need not be elaborate in its presentation. It should be thorough enough to convince the lender that you know who your customers are and show that you have charted a direction of how and what you are going to do to capture your company's share of the business market.

In terms of the business ask yourself:

1. *who you are*
2. *what you do*
3. *for whom you do it* (your targeted customer group)
4. *Why you do it* (what is your purpose or goal of accomplishment)

Your company's *goals* should encompass your long-range expectations of your desired results. Your *business strategies* should outline how your company is going fulfill its goals. Your *objectives* should be distinct and measurable points for accomplishment of your goals. You must also indicate what strides you will take to ensure your performance of certain elements and in what designated period of time you estimate completion.

NOTES:

"I" *is for*: IDEA

Conceived by desire, an *idea* begins as a minuscule seed. Planted in one's mind by a conscious or unconscious thought, it grows. Nurtured by endurance and nourished by initiative it feeds in the womb of creativity and slowly takes on a life of its own. It gains its strength from determination and drive until it comes to full term. Then, encouraged by the words of those who are endeared to it, the "idea" is born unto the world as a mental vision of a plan to be acted upon...

NOTES:

📁CHAPTER 9

DECISION MAKING:

A PSYCHOLOGICAL APPROACH

Choosing Your Business Name & Creating Your Business Image

You may ask, "What's in a business name?" Well, let me tell you that there is more to your company name than you might think. Choosing the right name for your business may actually play an important role in your company's success or failure. Why? It has to do with *Psychology* –the study of human behavior.

Whether or not you realize it, psychology plays a major role in our every day life. It doesn't matter if you are a business owner, a retail sales clerk, a secretary, a real estate agent or a landscaper; psychology plays a role in both your business life as well as your personal life.

Sigmund Freud's (1856-1939) psychological view of personality embraced his belief that behavior is the product

69

of everything that has happened to a person in his or her life from the time they are born. This includes emotional blocks, traumas and even fixations. These fixations are the dynamics that lead to what is sometimes called "games people play".

If Freud's view of psychology is believed, then it may explain why some people act one way in a given situation and others act in another way in the same situation. Because people are different and will act in different ways, the trigger that motivates them to do or not do, to respond or not respond, to act or not act to certain things will also differ. Acknowledging these differences and trying to understand which trigger to activate in order to motivate them to take the action you would like them to take is very important. The greater your understanding of personality and human behavior, the easier it will be to interact with others.

Your company's name conveys a mental image to the public at large. Based on the name, and how each individual perceives it, the image could be positive or negative. Before choosing your name, answer the following questions:

1. Who is *my* market group?

   A.   Adults (what age group, what socioeconomic level, what level of education, male or female)

   B.   Children (male or female, what age group, elementary school age, teenagers)

   C.   Specific group of people (crafters, dancers, artists, baby-boomers, retirees)

2. How do *I* see the company image I want to create?

   A.   Happy and whimsical (fun)

   B.   Business and very professional (corporate)

   C.   Warm and fuzzy (playing to people's emotions)

   D.   Clever and unique (creative)

   E.   Conventional (basic necessities)

   F.   Service-oriented (convenience)

   G.   Specialty (seasonal, appealing to certain groups of people only)

   H.   Sense-related (sight, smell, sound, taste, touch)

   (Examples: eye wear, perfume, music, food service/restaurants, and clothes)

3. What image do I want other people to "see" when they hear or see my company's name?

Once you've answered the three questions presented above, you will then want to ask yourself whether or not you want some portion of your company name to reflect the type of business in which you are engaged. This would offer you an "instant" advertising opportunity, in addition to giving your prospective customers a clue to your products or services. If you were a florist, maybe you would choose the name "Petal Pushers" (this comes to my mind because flowers obviously have petals). I'm sure you'll agree the name gives prospective customers a pretty good idea what the business is all about. Now that you understand the concept, let's talk about *customers* and *image* once again.

Giving your customers a clue to your products or services is an option available to you and it is the first step in this psychological process. Next, you want to be sure that your company name (whatever you choose) produces a visionary image within the customer group *you* want to reach.

Again, I offer some hypothetical examples to illustrate what I am telling you. All of the business names noted herein are fictitious in that they are a product of my mind created by me for this book for the sole purpose of helping me get my messages across to you.

Example #1: Your company sells snack foods and leases snack vending machines. You want to capture the corporate clientele. In your opinion, which of the two business names below best conveys an image to which a corporate business could relate: "Annie's Snacks & Vending Machines" or "Corporate Snacks & Vending Services"? The answer, in my opinion, is "Corporate Snacks & Vending Services".

Example #2: The hypothetical restaurant named "Mamma's Place" would make me think of a family-oriented, neighborhood eatery with good food and reasonable prices.

The name doesn't really tell me what type of food is being served (Italian, Mexican or...), but that's okay. It still gives me a visual image of the restaurant. The name evokes nostalgia; thoughts of delicious homemade food and a pleasant eating experience. "The Italian Cucina" may bring to my mind a slightly upscale, trendy Italian cafe with mid-range prices; while "IL Gusto Italia" makes me think of a high-dollar dining establishment featuring expensive wines, gourmet Italian food and rich desserts.

Example #2 talks about restaurants, but of course, the example can apply to any type of business. The important thing to remember is that if your business is aimed at targeting families and you want to let them know your prices are extremely affordable etc., then your name should convey that image (i.e. Mamma's Place).   But, if your establishment is more trendy, more expensive, or is not really geared for a family eating experience; the name "Mamma's Place" would be sending a message to the wrong group of people. There is more in a name than you may think. Make the right choice for your business.

Creating Your Company's Logo

Now that you've chosen your company name you've got to think about how you will go about building your company's image. The image you choose to convey will reflect your company's philosophy (your ethics and business rules and the way you feel your business should operate).   One way to create your company's image is through visual imagery and the use of a business logo. There are many large corporations that have logos that are easily identifiable even if their names do not appear next to their logo. One example that comes to mind is the apple logo with the bite taken from it which belongs to Apple Computers.

Graphic artists and free lance desktop publishers can help you create a logo for your business. Their prices will vary depending on their expertise and the complexity of your logo project. Your telephone company's yellow pages directory will help you identify and contact these professionals.

If your start-up business budget will not support such an expense, create your own logo yourself or with the help of a friend or relative who is artistically inclined. The design need not be elaborate, but in some way it should help tell the public what your business is all about.

Tools of the Trade

Understandably, you will want to limit your start-up spending while getting the most for your start-up dollars. However, there are certain things you will want to have in place initially to help transition your business from a start-up venture into a smooth and efficient moneymaking business operation. No matter what type of business you enter, you will need basic "tools of the trade" to begin—letterhead paper, business cards, facsimile cover sheets. In addition, there may be other materials needed based upon your individual business (i.e. restaurants will require menus, other businesses may require price lists, informational brochures). At a glance, these business tools must be able to communicate subliminal, as well as practical, information to your customers.

Letterhead - The basic components of your letterhead should include:

1. Company name and logo

2. Company address

3. Telephone and facsimile numbers

4. A brief statement or "motto" representing your business philosophy may also be included.

Although you may think it to be a simple task to create a letterhead design based upon the four items noted above...think again. The design must present a pleasing and balanced picture to the eye. The "style" of the picture will be created through the use of various font types and font sizes. Different font types will project different images to the beholder. Some type fonts can present a whimsical image to the eye, while others seem to relate to the "child" or the child within us. Scripted letters can convey the feeling of emotion or nostalgia, while other fonts are very business-like and rigid in their appearance. Decide who your targeted market group is to be and then determine what font style would best represent your business image.

The size and placement of your logo, your company name, address and telephone/facsimile numbers, and your motto, as well as print color, paper finish, paper texture and paper weight will all work together to create your business image. It is important to make sure that all these factors blend compatibly to create the proper image you want to convey. If any of these components are ill chosen your page "picture" will appear visually out of balance to the reader.

Business Cards

The business card is a form of advertising. The standard 31/2" x 2" card contains the name, address, telephone and facsimile numbers of the business as well as the individual's name and title. Often the card incorporates the company's business logo and a "motto" statement that indicates the types of goods or services handled by the company. Designed to say as much about the company and individual as possible within the confines of a very small space, the business card is a challenge to create. It is important to ensure that the logo and text will not appear too busy or crowded and that the placement of the words and logo offer enough space to maintain the balance necessary to create a pleasing visual picture. Likewise, color and texture of your card, as well as the font type and font size must be compatible with the image you want to convey.

Facsimile (Fax) Cover Sheet

A "fax" transmittal page is more than just a cover sheet for documentation you are sending to another company or individual. Think of it as yet another opportunity to advertise your company and tell others who you are and what you represent.

The fax sheet should contain your business name and logo, business address, telephone and fax numbers. The following information should be made part of the form:

1. Date the fax is being sent
2. Time of transmittal
3. Number of pages being transmitted, inclusive of the fax sheet
4. Name and telephone/extension number of the person receiving the fax
5. Name and telephone/extension number of the person sending the fax

6. Message space to indicate what is being sent and the reason for the transmission

When looking at the page, this document and all others you create, should present a pleasing picture of balance and style in a manner consistent with the professional look you want to capture and have your customers recognize.

NOTES:

"J" *is for*: JOURNAL

Keeping a business journal to track daily business happenings and conditions as they relate to variable situations can help you assess your overall business operation and predict the likelihood of upward spirals or downward dives.

> When my husband and I owned our liquor and junior market stores, we recorded any and all information in a given day that we felt may have been important as a means of future reference. Over time, our journal entries revealed:
>
> 1. Cigarette sales remained constant throughout the year.
>
> 2. The warmer the weather, the more beer and soft drinks we sold.
>
> 3. Sales of alcoholic beverages increased dramatically during the winter holiday season.

4. Our revenue intake was always higher on the day before a major sports event (like the World Series games, Super Bowl or televised boxing matches).

5. Food and grocery sales were higher right before any holiday or major sports event.

6. Bulk or boxed candy sales increased on Valentine's Day, Mother's Day, and during the Halloween season.

7. Revenue intake was always higher on days closest to the 1st and the 15th of the month (people were more apt to get paid on these days).

8. Revenue intake decreased on rainy days.

9. Revenue intake generally decreased within a month of Income Tax Day (April 15).

10. Certain foods and brand names of liquor, beer and soft drinks sold better than others did due to preference, ethnicity and age of our regular customers.

Documenting this information helped us guide our operation more efficiently and cost effectively. We were then able to "plan ahead" and buy more or less of food, alcoholic beverages and incidentals based on trends. By doing so we purchased more of the items that sold well and cutback, or even discontinued certain products that were not big selling items.   This strategy streamlined our operation and maximized our revenue.

The same journal-concept can be applied to any type of business.   Use it to determine if your business follows certain trends based on seasons, holidays etc. The journal can also be applied to advertising campaigns to determine the effectiveness of your advertising efforts. Write down: *the name of the publication in which the ad was placed, the date, day of the week, how many days it appeared in print, what the advertisement was trying to sell, the increase percentage of sales gained as a result of the ad, the specific products and services purchased as a result of the ad. . . . .* The knowledge you obtain in this manner can be invaluable to the success of your business operation. Remember: "J" *is for* Journal!

NOTES:

📁CHAPTER 10

TAKING ACTION

I must reiterate that going into your own business is both a big commitment and a big responsibility. Focus on being organized. Do your research to learn of your local and state government business requirements. Then take action! Visit the necessary offices and get all the paperwork ahead of time. I must credit my husband, who works for a governmental agency dealing with building trades, for the following quote: "Poor planning on your part, does not constitute an "emergency" situation on my part." His words leave little doubt that it would be unrealistic to wait until the eleventh hour to visit local governmental agencies and expect them to issue today what you as the customer needed "yesterday". Planning ahead will offer you the assurance that you will not get caught up in such a scenario. There will be forms to fill out and have notarized prior to actually securing the licenses. As a result, you will want to take care of these preliminary items first and then go back another day to actually secure your licenses and pay the required fees.

Business License

Find out which agency in your town or city issues business licenses and initiate a telephone call to determine the proper procedure for obtaining the license. The business license office should also be able to tell you the step-by-step procedure to follow to obtain any and all licenses required as well as where to obtain them. Depending on where you live, you may be required to get both a county business license and a city license.

The Fictitious Firm Statement

Often referred to as a "DBA" (Doing Business As) form, the procedure and fee for filing such a statement will vary depending upon the state in which you live. Some states require that you place a posting in a business newspaper publication for three weeks to make public notice of your intent to do business under a specific business name. Other states have you file a Fictitious Firm Name statement with the County Clerk's office. In this instance the Clerk's office can perform a search for you to ensure that no other business is operating under the same name. To determine what office in your city or town would handle such transactions, use your local telephone book to find the telephone numbers of your local government offices.

State Tax Certificate

If you are selling a taxable product, you will need to secure a state sales/use tax certificate from your state's department of taxation. Your business category will determine the fee. Some states will require that you remit collected sales tax on a monthly basis, while others may require quarterly or yearly payment. The department will explain all reporting procedures to you. Contact your telephone book for the telephone number and location of your local state office.

Other Licenses and Certificates

Depending on your type of business, other licenses and certificates (including proof of insurance) may be required. As an example, if you are hiring employees you will need a state business license and will be expected to carry worker's compensation insurance. You will also be required to obtain an Employer Identification Number (EIN) from the Internal Revenue Service. Businesses, which hire employees, are responsible for paying federal unemployment tax . . . .

A restaurant will need to obtain health department certificate for doing business. A liquor store will need a special state license to sell alcoholic beverages. Childcare providers must also be licensed to do business. Special licenses may take a significant amount of time to secure. It is up to you to take responsibility for meeting all these obligations in a timeline that will ensure that your business will open per your schedule.

"K" *is for*: **KNOWLEDGE**

Knowledge is information realized

Through lived experiences or from the written page.

It is the insight acquired over time;

The confidence that comes with age.

NOTES:

🗁 CHAPTER 11

WORKING WITH GOVERNMENTAL AGENCIES

Are you thinking of leasing a site in a strip mall? Or, perhaps you are seriously considering the idea of building your business structure from the ground up? In either case you can choose to work directly with an architect or engineer, or secure the services of a general contractor to create a set of building plans. Once again, fees for this will vary from state to state and architect to architect.

Tenant Improvement Space

The building plans will denote architectural, structural, plumbing, electrical and mechanical areas. Once completed your building plans must be submitted to the Plans Check section of your county government's building department. Upon approval, the agency will issue the building permit for your project. The main building permit will usually include the architectural plans. The cost of the permit is based on the size of the structure in relationship to the specific interior details (structure and the types and amount of electrical, plumbing and mechanical features therein), the category of your business and the intended use of the building. Once the building permit has been issued, the construction can begin. In addition, separate building permits will be required for each specific trade.

As a small business owner, you will probably choose to work with a general contractor. The general contractor will go out to bid for the sub-contracts for the various trade works to be done. When each phase of construction is completed, local governmental inspections are required to be performed by the respective trade areas (structural, architectural, electrical, plumbing, mechanical). Once inspected and approved, each designated inspector will sign-off (on a written record) for that portion of the work. The cost of the inspections is usually calculated into the cost of the permit. However, disapproval of any work completed within a phase will require more inspections. As a result, additional fees may be charged.

The type of business you engage in will determine whether or not other agency inspections may be required.

For instance, the fire department would inspect the cooking hood installation in restaurants as well as the overhead sprinkler system. A building designed as a senior citizens home would require fire department inspection, not only the overhead fire sprinkler system, but also the fire alarm system and the fire rating of the building plus any hazardous contents or equipment relating to the use of the building. Likewise, the health department would also inspect restaurants and other establishments falling under the jurisdiction of their code requirements. Federal laws, like The Americans with Disabilities Act, may also be applicable to your business so be sure you check into this as well.

When all the work is completed and approved, the governing governmental agency (county or city) will issue to you a Certificate of Occupancy which then entitles you to move into your space and begin your business operations.

New Construction

Buildings that are constructed from the ground up will also require architectural plans. However, prior to submitting these plans to Plans Check, the plans would first be directed to Zoning to determine whether or not they conform to laws relating to street curbs, street setbacks, driveways, alley access . . . Public Works would also have to review the plans for code conformance to utility hook-ups.

Guidelines for each phase of trade work would be applicable to those discussed under "Tenant Improvement Space". A Certificate of Occupancy would be issued when the building is completed and all inspections have been approved.

"L" is *for*: LEADER

Most of us realize our world is made up of two kinds of people: leaders and followers. The roles of both, the leaders and the followers, are necessary to provide continuity and balance to all aspects of our daily lives. While followers often have their own views and opinions of matters and sometimes will share them, they usually do not want to be placed in a position of authority. Rather, they are content to stand in the background and carry out the ideas, beliefs and directions of the appointed leader of the group.

Those of us who are "born" to lead are another matter entirely. Always eager to share their views and opinions, this personality type is most willing to assume an authoritative role. People with leadership capabilities share similar traits encompassing: initiative, determination, drive, perseverance, creativity, attention to detail, good judgment. . . Leaders are not content to be passive. Assertive and forthright, they often embrace rather than fear change.

Leaders are usually visionaries who look at the big picture and try to find alternatives to possible problem areas <u>before</u> such areas escalate to become crisis situations.

Are you a *leader* or a follower? The role of a leader is not to be taken lightly nor should it be envied. The leadership role is burdened with responsibilities, plagued with stress, complicated with problems and cursed by deadlines. Yet, in spite of all this, those willing to meet the leadership challenge head-on will not be deterred.

☐ CHAPTER 12

MARKETING

*Marketin*g encompasses the total activities by which goods or services transfer from the seller to the buyer: advertising, shipping, warehousing and selling. The act of marketing can be a single or collective coordinated effort by a person or persons formulated to reach a specific goal. Marketing campaigns often target designated groups of people for the purpose of persuading those groups to take action...the result of which would result in the sale of the goods and/or services offered by the marketer or his client. Marketing strategies are designed to make the targeted group:

1. Recognize, by name, the company being marketed. This can be achieved by using a business logo as the visual identifier that the customers see over and over again and will eventually remember. Recognition can also be effected

in the packaging color and style of a specific product or through use of a slogan or other type of advertising. (How many of you can ever forget the words "Where's the Beef?" or "Mikey Likes It!")

2. Identify with the company's business image, product or service.

3. Understand what is being offered. Whether the customer verbalizes his feelings or not, he is always asking "what's in it for me?" Your marketing campaign must help him to clearly see the advantages of your products or services.

4. Act in accordance to what your marketing strategy details. You must tell the potential customer what you want him to do: "Call this telephone number now" or "Return this reply card immediately", or "Don't delay, send for your free catalog today".

"M" is for: MAY (versus CAN)

I remember back to one night when I was a little girl sitting at the dinner table...

I asked my mother if I could be excused from the table so that I could go out and play with my friends.

"Can I be excused?" I asked excitedly.

"May I be excused?" My mother answered.

I looked at my mother inquisitively and waited for some type of explanation. "I thought I had already asked to be excused," I said to myself. Finally, she looked at me and said, "You want my permission to go outside so you have to say *may* I be excused, not *can* I be excused." I thought about this for a moment. *I'm just a little kid*, I whined to myself. *May...can? Yeah, whatever...* I decided I would do *whatever* it took as long as I could go outside and play. *"May* I please be excused?" I asked the question again. This time it worked. My mother said "yes" and off I went. A lesson learned? *May*be, but *may*be not.

I didn't really understand the meaning of *"can"* and *"may"* until I got a little older. *May* is an auxiliary verb that means, "to be permitted". When someone asks, "<u>may</u> I", he or she is really asking for permission. *Can* is an auxiliary verb that means "capable; having the ability". When someone asks, "<u>can</u> I"; he or she is questioning their own ability or capability to achieve.

> *May you do it? Yes, if you can.*
> *But can you do? If it's in your plan.*
> *"May or can"; what to do, what to do...*
> *You'll find the answer is up to you!*

So, if you should find yourself caught up in the "Mother, *may* I" dilemma, don't be torn between *may* and *can.* Tell yourself you have the power to achieve whatever you want to achieve. To succeed in whatever you want to accomplish, you don't need permission from anyone—but yourself! *May*be today is <u>your</u> month of "May" and this is your "May Day". *May*be it's true, that success is there for all who are willing to put forth the effort. Give yourself permission to live your dream and realize your true potential. Why? Because, in your heart—you <u>know</u> you "can"!

NOTES:

🗁 CHAPTER 13

ADVERTISING

The purpose of advertising is to induce people to buy your business's products or services by calling public attention to these products and services. Your company may offer the best products and services in the world, but without a means of reaching your targeted customer group, your business has little chance of success. Marketing and advertising is critical, especially when your business is new, because you are trying to establish your business niche. The type of business in which you engage and your targeted customer group will determine how much or how little advertising you will require. Accordingly, as your reputation and customer base grows, you may not need to spend as much on advertising. Established businesses revel in "word of mouth" advertising from repeat customers, feeling this form of advertising affirms success like no other.

Advertising can take on many different forms, which may include, but not be limited to, the following:

1. Billboards and Signs
2. Brochures
3. Catalogs
4. Coupons
5. Direct Mail packages
6. Invoice Inserts
7. Flyers
8. Magazine advertisements
9. Newsletters
10. Newspaper advertisements
11. Press Releases and public relations kits
12. Radio commercials, television and videos (because these three types of advertising media are high-dollar options and are not easily afforded by newly formed businesses, I will not be discussing them in this book).
13. World Wide Web

Billboards and Signs

Billboard advertising may be too costly for most new business owners to consider, but signs can be very affordable, especially magnetic signs. These signs are designed to be placed on the doors of your automobile, truck, or van. Whether you are driving your vehicle in the course of business or using it for personal pleasure, these signs provide continual advertising no matter where you travel. In addition, these signs can be easily removed from you vehicle and reapplied again at your discretion.

Brochures

Brochures are only restricted by one's creativity, there are no specific sizes or styles to which one must conform. My favorite brochure format consists of one piece of 8 1/2" by 11" paper folded into thirds creating a tri-fold brochure.

The customer's first point of contact with your image will be based on your company name, logo, company's address, telephone number and facsimile number and the visual picture created by the font style and size you choose to represent them. The *image* you create and present to the public at large through your brochures, or any other marketing and advertising piece, will be governed in part by your budget and will also be formed by your choice of paper: weight, color and finish, as well as font style, choice of print color(s) and the use of photographs or graphics.

Brochures can be created to focus on various components of your business as noted below. However, if the information you present does not clearly let your prospective customer know what's in it for them and what action you want them to take, your brochure will fall short of its goal.

1. <u>Company Overview Brochure</u> – introduces your company to the reader, it may include your company's purpose and mission statement, what makes your company a credible force in its chosen marketplace and a brief synopsis of what your company has to offer prospective customers in the way of products and/or services.

2. <u>Product/Service Overview Brochure</u> – provides general information about the products and services your company offers.

3. <u>Product/Service Specific Brochure</u> – This type of brochure focuses on specific products and/or services your company offers and goes into detail about them.

Because products and services may change from time to time, brochures written from a "general" perspective have a longer life and are more cost-effective to produce. With this in mind, you may choose not to create a brochure about specific products or services and instead produce a product sheet. The product sheet, usually formatted on an 8 1/2" by 11" piece of paper, can be revised more economically.

Catalogs

Catalogs are a larger version of a brochure. They usually contain multiple pages, are more product-oriented and contain detailed information and numerous photographs depicting the goods being offered. Catalogs are frequently produced using multiple pieces of 8 1/2" by 11" paper folded in half and staple-bound in place. The paper stock is often glossy white. The finish of the paper provides a high degree of resolution allowing for a sharper image of text, photography and/or graphics. The end result produces and conveys to the targeted market group an image of professionalism. Catalog covers are sometimes printed on a heavier weight of paper than are the information pages.

Coupons

Coupons are *active* pieces of written communication inasmuch as they provide the opportunity for the reader to move forward from the passive stage of just "reading" to the "doing" stage. A coupon can be used to direct the reader to fill it out and mail it back to you for more information about your company and its products and services. Not only are you telling the reader what to do, but also their action of providing their mailing information on your coupon also gives you a more tangible edge in reaching your targeted market group. The reader is no longer an unknown face in "zipcode" land, he or she now has a name and an address which you can include on your mailing list for future marketing campaigns.

People like to get free items and coupons can be used to provide them with "freebies" of some sort as a way of getting them to **act** and visit your business location. Coupons can also advertise "free" product drawings or discounted merchandise, which is still directed at leading the public to your business's front door.

The size of your coupon should be large enough to state its message and purpose, without being cumbersome. Be sure you provide easy directions for filling out the coupon and explicit information regarding redeeming any values as stated on the coupon. The expiration date and pertinent terms of the offer being made should also appear on the face of the coupon.

Direct Mail Packages

Direct mail is appropriately labeled. It sets a direct aim to the target group, which is why it can be so effective. Most direct mail pieces contain an outside envelope, a return envelope, a personal letter, a brochure and an order form. Some businesses have used a self-mailer rather than the two envelopes and re-engineered the rest of their piece to fit that design. At some point in time, you may want to experiment to see what works best for you. In the meantime, focus on the most important element of direct mail advertising—"your message". What you have to say and the way you structure your words to get your point across to the readers is the most critical aspect of getting them to take the action you specify.

Invoice Inserts

We've all received some type of bill or invoice that contained an advertising insert. In my local area, utility bills sometimes include 2-for-1 meal coupons or similar advertisements. Although the rate may be inexpensive for this type of advertising in relationship to other types, you will have to contact the companies in your area to get the details and find out the minimum amount of inserts that they will allow you to send. Utility companies reach large groups of people on a monthly basis so this form of advertising makes sense, but if large quantities are involved, this option may still be too expensive for your particular operation to utilize. If the large companies are out of your budget range, contact mid-sized companies.

Make an effort to agree on a financial arrangement that would be equitable to both of you.

Flyers

Flyers, usually sized to be either 8 1/2" " x 11" or 5" x 7", can be distributed in a number of ways. If you are willing to pay someone (a teenager or relative) to pass them out, people have been known to deliver them door-to-door in a specific geographic location. I've also seen them placed on cars in mall or grocery store parking lots. Also, look in your yellow pages for companies that specialize in delivering flyers.

Small local papers sometimes offer advertisers an incentive for running ads in their paper by making the offer to deliver the advertisers' flyer along with the newspaper for just a few pennies per flyer. By taking advantage of such an opportunity, you are able to target and reach a large segment of the population effortlessly. As a result this form of advertisement is not only functional, but it can also be cost effective.

Magazine Advertising

The white, coated paper used by most magazines supports the high-quality image of an upscale editorial environment which is one reason that magazine advertising rates will be more expensive than many other types of advertising. These rates will also tend to vary from magazine to magazines. Magazine advertising works well for many businesses, especially those national businesses that are large high-dollar operations. But, this advertising media is not for all businesses. There is a substantial "lag time" between the time the ad is placed and the time the ad appears. Consequently, if this is an issue with your business, you might better be served through other types of advertising, including local newspaper advertising.

Newsletters

A newsletter's main purpose is to communicate and it can do so effectively serving multiple purposes. With the many computer-aided programs available today, more businesses than ever can take advantage of this valuable tool, not just to disseminate information to the masses, but as an effective marketing tool designed to target and reach prospective customers and clients. Newsletters are discussed in greater detail in Chapter 14.

Newspaper Advertisements - Classified

Costs for classified advertisements are usually based on how many lines/words are in the ad and how many days you want the ad to run. The cost increases if you include graphics, bold headlines, or add lines of white space between your headline and your text. Call the classified department of the newspaper and obtain all the specifics relating to this form of advertising.

When you are ready to place an ad, you will probably want to write a draft copy to determine how you would like it to read. Once you see your ad on paper, you can rewrite it until it meets with your approval. Keeping the ad copy in front of you when you speak on the telephone to the classified ad representative will make it easier for you to convey the information to him/her.

On my draft copy, I always write the name of the newspaper in which I place: the ad, the date I call, the name of the person I speak to, the cost they quote me and the dates the ad will appear. If changes are made as we speak, I am sure to note them on my draft sheet. When the ad is published in the newspaper, I cut it out, attach it to my draft sheet and file it. Should I decide to run the same ad again in the future, I have all the pertinent information available to me. In the long run, this administrative act saves me both time and money.

Newspaper Advertisements – Display

Contact the major newspapers in your area and inquire about small business advertising rates for ads. Most newspapers will let you submit your own camera-ready ad as long as it conforms to their advertising guidelines. If you do not have the inclination or means to do this on your own, the newspaper's advertising representatives can assist you in designing advertisements that will accommodate your budget and convey your business image. Advertising rates are based on size of your ad based on inches and column width (full-page, half page, quarter page . . .) and will incorporate other factors including the use of graphics and/or color.

Newspaper - Feature Article

If your business or service is unique or somehow unusual, you may want to call your newspaper and tell them: *why* your business is so different from the rest, *what* exactly you are offering, *who* would benefit from your product or services, *when* and *how* you developed your business idea and *where* your business is located. If the paper agrees that such a story would appeal to its readers, they might agree to feature your business in an upcoming news edition. This "free" form of advertising provides you with yet opportunity to introduce your business to potential customers. Sometimes opportunity is only limited by your own creativity and initiative. Don't wait for opportunity to knock at your door; go out and find it.

Press Releases

Following the "who, what, why, where, when, and how" rule of journalism, a *press release* tells its story within the confines of only a few paragraphs. Often the entire story can be summed up in the first sentence and elaborated upon in the few paragraphs that remain. A press release may announce merger plans between two companies, inform readers of the appointment of an individual to a high-level position within an organization, or describe the upcoming events of a non-profit organization. It is a good way to keep your business name before the public's eye.

Public Relations Kits

Press release kits, designed to present to the media and other designated business people, are a means of touting new products and services being offered by your company. The "kit" is usually presented in a folder (or "package" of your choice) in which you will find a general press release about the new products as well as individual product information sheets, price sheets and other related information.

NOTES:

"N" *is for*: NICHE

It is important in life for everyone to find their own *niche* (a place or position where one best fits). Some people may find their niche working for a large corporation in the private sector, others may feel most comfortable as an employee of a small company; some may even choose public service in city, county or state government. Some people never find their niche. Instead they try to adapt and adjust. Unfortunately, it's like trying to put a square peg in a round hole; the fit just can't be made to "fit".

All of us enjoy certain chores, hobbies or school subjects better then others. Likewise, all of us perform certain tasks better then others. Knowing what we like or dislike, knowing the areas for which we have an aptitude versus those for which we are not well suited and discovering what we want to achieve in life will serve us well in helping us find our niche.

The first step in finding your niche is to ask yourself:

1. "What do I like to do and what do I do best?

2. "What are my goals?"

3. "What do I really want to accomplish in my life?"

Once you've answered these questions, write your goals down on a piece of paper. Next, set your objectives and list your strategies for meeting all your objectives. If you complete this exercise and realize you are not where you want to be, do whatever it takes to change this fact. If you complete this exercise and discover you've already found your niche, then I applaud you. After all is said and done, your niche is any place or any position that you feel is the right fit for you!

☐ CHAPTER 14

NEWSLETTERS

In its most simplistic form a newsletter offers its readers the opportunity to gain knowledge as it disseminates information to educate, enlighten and sometimes amuse its readers. Used effectively it can be fine-tuned to promote customer awareness of a business, pique interest in products or services, increase employee productivity by boosting employee morale, inform group members of upcoming events. . . When focused as a marketing tool, a newsletter can guide prospective customers into taking the action your company wants them to take. But, don't assume they will know this without being told; you will have to spell it out for them—"in writing" so your intent cannot be mistaken (i.e. _call_ this number today, _write_ for more information, _fax_ your inquiries to…).

It's true that anyone can create a newsletter, but producing a _successful_ newsletter is another matter entirely.

So, what makes a successful newsletter? My criteria for success would be this: 1) your newsletter captures and holds the reader's interest, 2) you're right on target with your publication's goals and 3) your newsletter gets results (you have business processes in place that can measure increased customer action directly attributable to your newsletter). Now that we've established your newsletter's objectives, let's look at what must be done in order to achieve them:

1. Identify your sales market group. Remember you are trying to reach prospective customers and in order to do so, you have to know which segment of the public at large you are trying to reach.

2. Focus on what it is that you want to accomplish:

a. Bring to the public the awareness of your company's existence.

b. Promote an image by which the public can readily identify your company. As the owner of the business, the power to create and promote your company's image is in your hands. Surprisingly, there are business owners who don't understand this so it bears repeating. Your business image can be projected through your company name and logo; the name of your newsletter; the look and style of your publication; the texture, weight and color of the paper you choose; the font style and size of your publication and the content and quality of your message and your written word.

c. Increase sales and revenue. Usually 80% of a company's business comes from 20% of its customers.

3. Develop the content of your publication. Your content will be the catalyst that will promote customer action—and customer action will make the sale.

The parameters of your newsletter budget will significantly determine the paper size, color, weight and overall look of your newsletter. However, there is no reason why you cannot stay within your budget and still produce the best newsletter your dollars will allow.

When I owned my writing business in California I produced an 8 1/2" by 11" newsletter monthly. It was tri-folded horizontally rather than vertically. The first outer-fold was used as a mailer indicating my business name and address in the upper left-hand corner and allowing enough room for the recipient's name and mailing address. The newsletters were targeted not only to small business owners, but also to corporate businesses addressed to many of my human resources peers.

The middle section of the outer page displayed my company name, the name of my publication and a sentence stating who we were (what kind of services were offered). The lower third of the outer page provided more detail about our goods and services. When the newsletter was opened my company name and newsletter name appeared at the top along with the month, year and volume number of the publication.

The rest of the 8 1/2" by 11" page consisted of two things: 1) an editorial written by me and indicating my by-line and 2) a piece that explained to the reader what my business had to offer them ("what's in it for them) and directed them to take action.

The editorial would be on a variety of subjects using the months of the year as a main theme and were not business-oriented. Guided by the month of each publication, the newsletter was printed on a different color paper each month (i.e. March might be *green* in conjunction with spring; April *yellow* representing Easter, October would be *orange* in honor of Halloween . . .).

My publication gave readers a chance to be distracted from business for a few minutes and be entertained, amused and/or enlightened. It also provided readers with an opportunity to discover my writing capabilities without realizing they were doing so. It takes about 3-4 times of receiving a direct mail piece for people to really identify with your company and your message and it was so rewarding for me to be out and about in a business setting and have people come up to me and say they enjoyed my latest newsletter.

As time went on, I expanded my newsletter from one 8 1/2" by 11" page to one 11" by 14" page which when folded in half created a 4 page publication. To offset the cost of producing the newsletter, I sold advertising space to local businesses. The partnering was successful in that it helped me pay for my publication and provided another source of advertising to these local businesses. Over time, the selling of ad space became a job in itself and the added burden of having to produce my own 4-page publication each month took valuable time away from meeting demands of my other clients for whom I produced newsletters. Upon re-evaluating the reasons for originally creating the newsletter, I determined that the 8 1/2" by 11" format to which I returned sufficiently and successfully met my marketing requirements.

Think of each blank page of your newsletter as a canvas upon which you will create your picture of words. To create a page that is visually pleasing to the beholder, your newsletter picture should reflect balance and harmony through text, color, graphics, photographs, font size and style and white space. You must also decide how you will format your page with respect to columns. Your page size will have a direct bearing on whether you use the single page format, the two-column format or the 3-column page, which gives the reader the feeling of reading a magazine or a newspaper. Publications that are overburdened with text will not grab the reader's attention. Photographs, graphics and article headings should be used to hook the reader into reading on, while white space can offer a "pillow of rest" for the reader to rest his or her eyes periodically.

Distributing Your Newsletter

Mailing Lists

You will want to include your present customers, suppliers and friends on your newsletter mailing list, but how will you reach the people that are unknown to you?

The answer is through the use of mailing lists. Trade or business organizations like the Chamber of Commerce often make their mailing lists available to others. Likewise companies that sell products that complement (but do not compete with) your own may also be willing to share their lists. Lists can be obtained from list brokers or directly from companies that specialize in making lists available for rent (these lists are not sold). Check the yellow pages under "Mailing Lists". Lists can be tailored to your requirements—by zip code, by geographic area, by income, by marital status, by gender. The following web site: http://www.yellow.com/ will allow you to "check out" the yellow pages online.

For more information about publicly accessible mailing lists, the Internet site: http://www..NeoSoft.com.internet/pam// is another resource available to you.

<u>Invoice Inserts</u>

Once you've made decisions about all the components of your newsletter, you will need to decide on the most cost-effective means of distributing your publication. Inserting your newsletter with each invoice you mail is one option to consider. A second option would be to contact other companies to determine if you can work up a mutually agreeable financial arrangement which would allow them to insert your newsletter into their invoice envelopes or other mailings.

Bulk Rate Mail Permit

Another suggestion is to obtain a bulk rate mail permit from the United States Postal Service. Be sure to check with the post office and find out all the parameters regarding this type of mail option. The rules and regulations are very specific and must be strictly adhered to with respect to bundling the mail and segregating the bundles by zip codes.

Networking

Your newsletter is an effective networking tool that can be handed out at business group gatherings, Chamber of Commerce meetings and any other opportunity for public interaction. Never leave home without them…

"O" is for: ORGANIZATION

Organization is a means of creating order and providing method to whatever we do. The ability to organize is the ability to maintain sequential arrangement of objects or tasks by implementing some sort of classification system.

The act of organizing objects follows the old adage "a place for everything and everything in its place". Organizing reduces clutter and saves time. Having a place for everything enables us to know exactly where a particular item is to be kept and reduces time spent looking for that item when it is called upon to be used again.

Organizing tasks helps categorize their importance and allows us to assign a priority order to their completion. The procedure of organizing and prioritizing tasks minimizes wasted efforts...it is one strategy of time management.

In today's fast-paced world of high technology, being able to handle more than one project at a time is a necessity. Good organizational skills are paramount to all aspects of your life, whether you utilize these skills in your work place, your personal life or in a social or recreational environment. It's never too late to get organized. Start now and discover the key role *organization* can play in _your_ life.

▭CHAPTER 15

NETWORKING

Networking is the act of communicating and interfacing with other people in an effort to establish mutual relationships which will help further careers or promote the business interests of all parties involved. The act of networking offers the opportunity of letting other business owners and professionals discover what your company has to offer. Enlightened with this knowledge they in turn will be able to talk to others about your business which increases your likelihood of adding to your customer base through these word-of-mouth referrals.

Chamber of Commerce Organizations

Chamber of Commerce organizations at the community, state and national levels are well known for supporting and advocating the businesses (both large and small) of its members. The organization offers a myriad of programs, activities and services which include, but are not limited to:

leadership classes designed to broaden perspectives and enhance the leadership skills of its participants, information about small business administration and small business insurance plans and business networking and referral opportunities. Membership fees may vary based upon city and state, community demographics, as well as business size and category.

Chamber of Commerce organizations usually hold monthly early-hour business breakfast meetings and/or "after five" evening mixers at which members get the chance to meet and mingle as they exchange business cards, build business liaisons and forge new friendships. In addition, monthly chamber of commerce luncheon meetings usually feature keynote presenters whose topics relate to business issues and business concerns shared by the majority of the membership. Designed as an information forum, these luncheon meetings usually allow time for a question and answer period.

Business showcase events and community business fairs are optional Chamber of Commerce events in which a business owner may want to participate. For a designated fee the business owner can purchase display space or booth space at one of these events and exhibit products or services to the community at large. These events provide the opportunity to meet members of the community on a one-on-one basis. The visibility your company gains through this type of participation gives you a solid foothold as a member of your local business community and helps to validate your business standing to the public.

Leads Groups

Contact your local newspaper or check the yellow pages for information about "leads" groups in your area. Most people like to do business with someone personally known to either themselves or a friend as it provides them with a greater sense of security that they will be treated fairly and competently. With this in mind, leads groups exist to provide a networking opportunity for business owners wherein they can tout their companies, exchange business cards, make new business relationships and each act as an avenue of referral for the other.

Many leads groups are structured in such a manner that they offer membership to only one business per business category. For instance, there would be only one florist, one jeweler, one insurance agent etc. This practice ensures that members will not have to compete against each other. If a group member gets a "lead" that someone he or she knows is looking for a florist, the lead is offered to the florist member. If the jeweler, knows someone who is looking for an insurance agent, he or she will pass on the prospective customer's name and telephone number to the insurance agent ...

Other Networking Groups

While "leads" groups are made up of members representing a variety of businesses and industries, there are other groups that represent specific businesses or industries (i.e. retail liquor stores associations, writers groups, paralegal groups, building contractors organizations. . .)

Networking groups may be designed to focus on a specific field like human resources, rather than a specific business or industry. While each member company may represent diverse industries such as aerospace, manufacturing, retail etc., the one common denominator they all share is dealing with human resources issues. In this scenario, networking would be focused on discussing issues and problems relative to the human resources field and exchanging ideas and solutions to shared mutual concerns. This type of group would share with its members: techniques on how to conduct more effective interviews, state and federal labor law updates, information on worker's compensation reforms and more. . .

Toastmasters International is a group designed to help its members hone their public speaking skills. Members are required to write speeches and present them in front of the group for critique. While this is the main focus of each gathering the meetings provide the opportunity to network, expand one's business relationships and tout one's business endeavors.

NOTES:

"P" *is for*: PERCEPTION

Offering no argument for dispute, reality is the totality of things and events that are confirmed and accepted to be actual. But if reality encompasses all that exists outside the mind, does this mean that life's reality is always so clear-cut as to never be mistaken? No, unfortunately this is not the case at all.

Just like the personal observations, mental images and physical sensations we experience and believe when we see and witness feats of magic, visions that seem apparent to one's own eyes are not always what they appear to be. Masked in the illusion of reality, an awareness or judgment of something that cannot be substantiated with tangible physical evidence is considered *perception*.

Often perception and reality are at odds with each other. Sometimes the perception of what is real may appear to be more real than the truth of the matter... When this is recognized, perception can be used in a positive way. We have the power to turn the *perception* of what is believed into the reality of what is actual.

I discovered the differences between perception and reality when I entered the field of real estate in the early part of the 1980's. In awe of those of my peers who drove Cadillacs and Mercedes and wore expensive clothes, I wondered if I would ever enjoy the same success as they so obviously did.

Eventually I learned that although many of my fellow realtors were moderately successful, they parlayed their success to a grander scale by believing in their success and living the part. Most of the expensive cars they drove were leased to give the perception of success. The expensive clothes, manicured nails and carefully coiffured hair further perpetuated the feeling and image of success. In this manner they used perception to their advantage. In time, the perception of their success contributed to their success until the perception and the reality balanced and were equal.

My real estate peers explained to me that the customers' opinion of the real estate agent is forming from the moment the would-be clients enter the real estate agency and see the agent. This client "appraisal" is being conducted based on the agent's appearance (looks, clothes, jewelry, hairstyle, nails, shoes etc.), mannerisms, voice tone and articulation characteristics and the confidence (or lack of confidence) the real estate agent exudes.

If the real estate sales agent is meeting at the homeowners' home in the hope of listing that property for sale, chances are the homeowners will keep watch through their window until they see the agent drive up. In this scenario, the appraisal of the realtor begins as soon as he or she exits their car and starts to walk up to the front door. The make, model and year of the car being driven by the agent is the first assessment being processed in the minds of the homeowners. If expensive car equates to success in the minds of many people, then this would help to form the perception of the individual's success.

In many ways, buying or selling a home is often an emotional experience. Likely, it is the largest monetary purchase that most people will make in their lifetime. With this thought in mind it is understandable that prospective clients, who are looking to buy or sell a home, want to feel comfortable that the agent with whom they work is competent, understands the real estate market and maintains a successful track record in the real estate field. This comfort zone provides them with a feeling of assurance that their agent will meet their real estate needs and effect the best possible results for them.

The more involved in real estate I became, the more I learned for myself that my co-workers were absolutely right with regard to perception versus reality. I could understand how leasing an expensive car could enhance one's career, but I never felt that success would elude me entirely if I chose not to lease. More importantly, what this learning exercise in perception and reality actually taught me is that psychology plays an important role in our everyday lives. Understanding the psychology behind why people do what they do in certain situations and learning how to utilize this information to its maximum advantage is that best way to ensure success.

I believe that to be successful, you must <u>think</u> success, <u>live</u> success, <u>dress</u> success, <u>act</u> success and <u>speak</u> success. Attitude is everything. Using perception to its best advantage *may* allow you permission to show the world how successful you are, but the reality of the matter depends on whether or not you <u>can</u> be successful. If you have the ability to succeed and the will to believe in yourself, then you will be successful. There's no perception about it. The reality of the matter is really quite simple... Dream it; see it; live it; be it! Make it happen for <u>YOU</u>.

NOTES:

☐CHAPTER 16

CUSTOMER SERVICE

The single most important focus of any business is the "customer" because without the consumer there would be no business. In spite of this plain fact, it is surprising how many business owners fail to neither realize the customer's true importance nor put any real effort into determining how they can best serve them. Customer service is vital to the success of any business. The best form of advertising is word of mouth advertising from repeat customers. Satisfied individuals who tout your products and services to others are worth their weight in gold.

So what constitutes good customer service? It's all about personal attention, going the "extra mile" and working to make each customer feel special. It is not only the act of listening to the wants and needs of the people who patronize your business, it is also making a conscious commitment to try to meet their needs. Remember that it's the shopping experience that counts! If the business staff was friendly and attentive and the memory of the experience was a good one, many times people will pay a few dollars more as opposed to going to the competitor's store where they can get the same items for less, sans the "service".

It's not really difficult to give good customer service, but not everyone does it well. Why? It takes effort! Unfortunately, most people are not willing to put forth the effort. The interesting fact is that it takes effort to accomplish *anything* worthwhile. The effort required to provide good customer service is minimal, yet the rewards to be realized are significant.

7 Easy Tips for Rendering Good Customer Service

Share your philosophy about good customer service with your staff. Provide them with adequate training to ensure they will be able to render the quality of service consistent with your expectations and your business culture.

1. Acknowledge the customer. Nothing gets the customer more upset than entering a place of business and not being acknowledged by a staff member. Even if you or your staff representatives are with another customer finishing paperwork from a previous transaction, or

speaking to a customer via telephone; most people will not mind the wait half as much if they are acknowledged.

2. First, S-M-I-L-E. Then speak in a friendly and courteous tone of voice when greeting the customers. Actions can speaker louder than words. To eliminate any miscommunication or misunderstanding between your business representatives and your consumers, ensure that their poise, stance, mannerisms and facial expressions are conveying to the customers the same language as their words are speaking (refer to Chapter 23 – Understanding Non-Verbal Communication).

3. Think of everyone who enters your business as a potential customer regardless of gender. Just as you would not want to judge a book by its cover do not judge the people who enter your business. As an example, if a man enters a woman's clothing store, he may be there to purchase something for his wife. Don't ignore him. If a man and woman enter a car dealership, focus should not be directed exclusively toward the man as if the woman were not there at all. She may actually hold the trump card that will determine whether or not the couple will actually make the specific purchase. In either of these examples, it would not be a good business practice to "miscalculate" your

potential customers. Treat them all equally and render to them the same degree of respect and courteous service.

4. Call repeat customers by their names. Everyone likes to hear the sound of his or her own name. Such a courtesy will reaffirm that you feel they are special to your business operation.

Make eye contact with your customer as he or she is speaking. This will let him or her feel that you are providing them with your undivided attention as they make their inquiries about your products or services. The personal touch will go a long way in securing a strong business-base of repeat customers.

5. Listen to what the customer is saying. This is especially true if they are upset and are trying to voice a concern either about a purchase they've made or about the interaction they've had with one of your staff members.

There will also be times when the customer will be agitated about something that has occurred prior to coming in to your establishment; however, something triggers them to vent at your staff member instead.

At times it will be difficult for you, or even for them, to know what they really want you to do for them. Frequently, they just want to verbalize their frustrations. Let them speak and maintain your eye contact with them. When they are finished, respond to them in a calm tone of voice and repeat to them what you think you heard them say. This technique indicates to them that you have been listening. As a result, they will usually begin to calm down a bit.

If you can remedy their situation, take action. However, there will be times when you cannot satisfy their requests or concerns. Although your customers may be disappointed, they will usually respect your reasons for not being able to take action as long as they feel you've been receptive, attentive and empathetic toward their problems.

NOTES:

"Q" *is* *for*: QUALITY

Quality is the degree of perfection to which a task or responsibility is performed. It is the exact specifications toward excellence to which a product is produced. Various industries and business fields have standards to which they adhere. These quality standards represent a blueprint to follow to get the job done and criteria to ensure the job will be performed in the same accepted manner each time.

Without quality measures how many medical operations would go awry? How many dollars would be deposited to the wrong bank accounts? How many other aspects of our daily routines would be critically affected? The consequences of such situations are overwhelming to contemplate.

Quality is paramount to our existence in ways that we may not have previously imagined. The ongoing assurance of quality in our lives demands conscientious thought and meticulous detail of action on a twenty-four hour basis, three hundred and sixty five days per year.   Unfortunately, many people tend to shirk this obligation with the attitude that someone else will do it.   But, if people were to perpetuate the thought that quality is not their responsibility, who will take responsibility for quality? What would happen if no one picked up the "quality" slack?

Quality-minded people adhere to a high caliber of personal and business ethics and take pride in their accomplishments, both personal and professional. They are detail oriented, sometimes to a fault. Whether you work for someone else or work for yourself, isn't it obvious that the accountability to quality belongs to everyone en masse, rather than just a random few?

I offer the following food for thought: *If there were no quality in life, there could be no quality of life.   If there were no quality of life, what would life mean?*   In my opinion, when it comes to the matter of quality; *quality* matters. That's why my A-B-C approach to business (and life) touts that "Q" *is for*: Quality.

🗁 CHAPTER 17

DRESSING FOR SUCCESS

Psychology is the study of human behavior and I am a devoted student of the science. Whenever I get the opportunity—sitting in the waiting room of my doctor's office, waiting in line at the post office or sitting in the lobby of a restaurant waiting for a table—I like to watch people. There is nothing as interesting as observing how people dress and noting how they behave in certain situations. I've often wondered what motivates us to dress the way we do. While the obvious reasons would be protection and comfort, I would guess that some of us dress to conceal added pounds and others of us dress to gain acceptance of, or identify with, our peer groups.

Whether or not we realize it, our mode of dress often provides others with a portfolio of information about us. Our clothes can indicate our social standing, our cultural status, our economic level, our level of sophistication and even our level of success. For the most part, I believe our choice of clothes really does mirror who we are, but sometimes when we look into our own mirror we might see a completely different picture then the one that others see when they look at us. It has been my observation that people frequently judge others on a first impression based on the other person's appearance. This may be either a conscious or subconscious act; but if we choose to be honest with ourselves, we will admit most of us have made this type of assessment at one time or another.

Appearance is a composite of many things: hair color, hairstyle, make-up, clothes, shoes; as well as, voice tone, voice volume and physical attributes. The way we dress sends signals to others about who we are—our values, our preferences, our attitudes. Our manner of dress may be sending out the right messages or even the *wrong* messages to the receiver without our being aware of the way they are being interpreted. In turn, others may actually be oblivious to the fact that our clothing styles are playing a part in their assessment of us. People tend to make evaluations based on senses and perceptive beliefs of what they see and hear. Right or wrong, this method of appraisal is quite common. You may not be able to change this type of evaluation, but you can learn to dress for success and make perception work to your advantage.

If we are to believe the old saying "clothes make the man", then there is no reason not to believe that clothes can also make the woman. Men and women, before you spend another dollar on clothes I suggest you take stock of yourself and then take inventory of the clothes in your closet. What type of image do you want to convey? Do you feel your present wardrobe reflects the image you see for yourself? What style of clothes would best befit the type of job you perform?

Different industries subscribe to different dress standards depending on the work being performed. What is appropriate for one industry might not be appropriate for another and visa versa. For instance, if you work in one of the building trades and spend a lot of time walking construction job sites, you don't want to wear a suit and expensive shoes that could get scuffed with every step you take. Most likely this style of dress would be prohibited from a safety standpoint as well. Although a very casual and comfortable look would be most appropriate, you don't have to limit your wardrobe to sweatshirts and blue jeans—unless of course that look has your name written all over it.

For a man or woman working in the business world, jeans and a sweatshirt would not be considered appropriate dress. In this type of environment you may be required to wear tailored suits or clothing styles that project your company's specific image whether that image is conservative, trendy, high-tech, or corporate. It may be somewhat easy to visualize the clothing styles appropriate to both the construction trades and the corporate business environment, but there are so many other industries and business fields that are not so clearly definable. If your particular field, or your employer, has not created a standardized business image, create your own image—for you.

I realized early on in my life that my own self-esteem elevated when I was dressed up as opposed to when I dressed in ordinary casual clothes. This is probably one reason that I sought and enjoyed every opportunity that allowed me to "dress-up". I also enjoyed (and still enjoy) wearing jackets. Jackets make me feel slightly more "dressed up" than if I were to wear just a skirt and blouse or just a nice pair of dress slacks and a blouse.

When I entered the business world for the first time, I had to decide what style of clothing I would wear. Without a doubt I knew I liked to dress up. It was acceptable by my industry and definitely appropriate for me to go to work in high-heeled shoes and dresses, or clothing ensembles (like suits) that included jackets. To stress to you how much more comfortable I felt being dressed up as opposed to dressing casually, I was twenty-one years old when I purchased my first pair of jeans. My then beau (and now husband of many, many years) had asked me to go hiking. I didn't think my high-heeled shoes and suits would be appropriate so I went shopping for jeans, specifically for the occasion. My husband, on the other hand, *is* a jeans and sweatshirt man and has always worked in a field where such clothes are appropriate attire. He hates to dress up and practically has a tantrum when he has to wear a suit.

We each spent many years trying to change the other's *style* of clothing and dress. I would try to convince him to purchase a more fashionable wardrobe and he would try to talk me into wearing jeans and sweatshirts more often. (I haven't owned a pair of jeans in many, many years).

One day we both came to an understanding that unless it was a wedding, black tie dinner, or camping trip where one absolutely had to conform to the dress code set forth, there was no reason why we each couldn't dress the way we felt most confident and comfortable. Of course that meant that I'd be wearing a suit or some type of jacketed outfit and high heeled shoes and he would be in some variation of the sweatshirt and jeans look. Sometimes he would "dress up" just a bit and wear colored jeans, but that was pushing it.

Whether it was the jackets themselves or just the added confidence that the jackets afforded me, I managed to climb the corporate ladder. Maybe I owe some of my success to perception and the part perception plays in altering reality. If you feel good about yourself and others sense that feeling, then they feel good about you too. If, through your demeanor, you are perceived as being professional and able to do the job, then that perception might work to your advantage and become the reality of the matter.

Another interesting aspect of perception came to light when I owned a writing service in California. I made a startling observation over the course of a month or two. Sometimes I would make deposits to my business bank account on a day when I was not actually working. Dressed in leggings or sweat pants and an oversized shirt, I would wait my turn in line until the merchant teller motioned for me to come forward. I would usually get a cursory smile and hello, but that was it. Pleasant, but not personal. However, on the days that I was all dressed up in a suit or jacketed outfit not only did I get a hello, but I was called by my name and given the personal treatment in a professional tone reserved for the bank's business customers. At first I thought it was my imagination.

I began to make written note of the days I went to the bank, what I was wearing and how the staff interacted with me. My journal notes indicated I was treated with a different measure of respect when I was dressed up as opposed to when I was not dressed up.

Dark clothes are "perceived" as having more authority. The ultimate sign of power for the male executive is symbolized in the black, 3-piece suit. Likewise, to perpetuate this real or perceived image of power and authority, a woman might then choose a navy blue or charcoal gray suit.

> My wardrobe always includes the basics: a dress, skirt, jacket and pair of slacks in black and navy for all seasons; and a dress, skirt and pair of slacks in beige for spring and summer. From these basics, I can add *color* and create a whole new look for business or any other occasion.

When introducing color into your wardrobe there are two things to consider: 1) Not everyone can wear every color of the rainbow to its best advantage, although most people can wear varying shades of all colors. Some colors tend to brighten our complexions and make our faces light up with a glow. Other colors can make us look pale, sallow, drab or just plain washed-out. If you are not sure what colors or shades look best on you, it may be worth the money to have a professional color coordinator do a color work up for you. Knowing what colors you wear well will help you coordinate your clothing purchases; 2) Not only can the colors we wear send conscious or unconscious signals to others, colors can have either a positive or negative effect on the receiver's mood.

• Red is considered a *hot* color. In a business setting red can be seen as an aggressive color; in a personal setting red can signal anger, excitement or even love (i.e. a *red* heart for Valentine's Day).

- Blue is a *cool* color. Viewed as pleasant and calming in a business setting, blue may even be thought of as tender or leisurely from a personal point of view.

- Yellow is a cheerful color, pleasant and spring-like. However, in reviewing "yellow" in retrospect, I must conclude that "yellow" doesn't wear well in the corporate environment.

- Green is also a *cool* color. Green, the color of nature, is soothing in any environment.

- Purple is often thought of as a regal color (as in the purple robes of royalty). In a business setting, purple is dignified and commands respect.

You don't have to spend big dollars on your wardrobe. You can dress nicely, convey the image you want to convey and still make your clothing purchases within your designated budget. Maximize your spending dollars and stretch your wardrobe by learning to mix and match your clothes to create additional outfits.

Pink, powder blue, or any pastel color tends to give me a washed out look. Vibrant colors tend to brighten my face. I look best in red and certain shades of green, as well as jewel-tone colors like teal, purple, and Cobalt blue. When I shop I know that I will choose clothing in these colors because they are flattering to my hair and complexion and I wear them well. This awareness gives me the confidence to know that I can match any item in my existing wardrobe with anything I buy to create another outfit and a new look. I never have to worry about matching my skirt with a blouse or coordinating my jacket to create that total look, as all my colors are compatible.

Accessorize your outfits to get even more value for your wardrobe dollars. Women, you can use scarves, jewelry and other accessories to create many different fashion looks. Adding a touch of both grace and style to your wardrobe, accessories can help you make a smooth and effortless transition from the office to the after hours business dinner meeting.

A scarf may be the accessory I choose to wear with a dress (sans the jacket) for a mid-day business meeting. If I remove the scarf, add an eloquent gold pin and matching earrings to my dress and perhaps put on a "dressy" jacket, I can leave my office just in time to make that 6 p.m. meeting.

See what the stores have to offer, then use your imagination and inventiveness to create a one-of-a-kind style that is undeniably you.

NOTES:

"R" *is for*: RESOURCEFUL

From the super highway of information called the Internet, to books, video tapes, seminars, classes, courses, networking groups and more, the quest for facts need not lead you down a dead-end street with no place to go. To be *resourceful* is to be able to recognize detours that may be impeding personal life goals or career objectives and then take action to work around these obstacles. A resourceful person is not content to follow the most obvious course to enlightenment. Instead he or she will venture off the beaten path in an effort to find short cuts that will lead to answers and knowledge.

Being resourceful is a bit like playing "private eye"... except today's detective doesn't have to spend hours pounding the pavement hunting for leads and bits of information. If you want to solve your life's mysteries, you must have a clue as to what you're looking for. Then you must be willing to go to do whatever it takes to find what you need. There are many avenues of knowledge available to those who are *resourceful* enough to seek them out. Are you are resourceful person? If you think you are, put yourself to the test. Unlock the powers of your mind. Let your creativity lead you; learn to think outside of the box. Be willing to follow up on data, be able to ask questions and be open to networking with others. In the long run, it doesn't matter whether or not you choose self-employment, stay in your present line of work or seek employment with a new employer. The important thing is to weigh your options, discover alternate ways of doing things, and find out what will make YOU happy. You can make the pieces of the puzzle fit by being ready and willing to gather information from any and all sources. Be open to the possibilities. You'll find the answers you need to help you ride down life's main thoroughfare towards the high road to success.

◻️CHAPTER 18

THE HUMAN RESOURCES
CONNECTION

Workers are considered *human resources*; but as it relates to businesses, "human resources" encompasses much more than just having people working for your company. Before we discuss the many aspects of human resources and your responsibilities as a business owner, let's focus on the subject of "workers".

A worker is someone hired to do a specific job that may involve expending physical or mental effort towards a focused goal and specified end. We will be discussing three different types of workers (employees, independent contractors, and temporary employees) in order to help you decide which type of worker will best serve your business operation.

EMPLOYEES

In an employer-employee relationship, the business owner (employer) controls the employee's work hours, work place, work schedule, the scope of the job to be done and the method by which the work will be performed and completed. *Control may be the determining reason in and of itself for a company to choose this manpower option. The downside may be the financial burden of responsibility it poses with respect to payroll taxes, and the expense of various insurance policies and premiums required maintaining this type of work force.*

Payroll Taxes

If your company decides to hire employees, you will need an Employer Identification Number from the Internal Revenue Service as you will be required to withhold social security, Medicare and federal income tax from the earned wages of each of your employees. As an employer, you must also pay your share of these taxes. In addition, some states have state income tax laws. If your state has such a law, state income tax must also be deducted from the employee's wages and your company will be required to pay your own portion of that tax, as well. If your budget will allow for the expense, there are independent payroll services that will handle the entire payroll task for your company.

Unemployment Insurance

Employers must contribute to their state unemployment insurance tax fund and pay a federal unemployment insurance tax. Employees terminated by your company due to lay-off or for reasons other than serious infractions of misconduct may apply for unemployment benefits. Through your contributions to this state fund, these monies are paid out to eligible ex-employees of your company.

Worker's Compensation Insurance

As an employer with employees, you must carry worker's compensation insurance and pay monthly premiums. In the event an employee sustains a work-related injury or sickness, compensation to eligible workers would be paid from these monies.

Other Insurance Premiums

Depending on your type of business, you may be required to carry additional insurance policies for liability, errors & omissions, etc.

Job Benefit Packages

Most employers offer some type of employee benefits, which include: health insurance, a retirement plan, vacation and sick time.

INDEPENDENT CONTRACTOR

The independent contractor is not considered your employee nor is he or she on your payroll roster. For this reason you will bear no responsibility for withholding taxes from his or her check, or for providing benefits of <u>any</u> <u>kind</u> (insurance, vacation, sick leave pay . . .) to the independent contractor. Another advantage is that the working relationship is "per the project" and is only to exist for a specified period of time. The downside to this option is that in a true independent contractor relationship, you have very little control over the person's time and working schedule. As long as the job gets done as set forth, you cannot dictate a step-by-step account of how or when the contractor will do the job.

The Internal Revenue Service has the final say in determining whether a worker is properly classified as an independent contractor or an employee. One factor to be considered is the *relationship* itself: 1) How is the working relationship perceived between you and the worker? 2) Does the worker conduct similar work for others? 3) Is the worker working on other client projects simultaneously? If the worker performs similar work for others, sets up his/her own working schedule and has the equipment necessary to perform such projects, it is probable that an independent contractor situation does exist.

Another factor to be considered is *control*: 1) Do you control how the person gets the project done? 2) Do you control the actual site location of where the job is to be performed? 3) Do you control or provide the specific type of equipment to be used? 4) Do you control the exact hours in which the work will be performed? 5) Is the relationship open-ended and not defined for a specific length of time? If you've answered *"yes"* to some or all of these questions, it is possible your relationship with your worker is that of any employer-employee.

The *financial* aspect is another to be considered. Is the worker performing the work accountable to his or her own non-reimbursed business expenses? Does the worker have his or her own equipment necessary for performing the job? If so, this will help to support independent contractor status.

TEMPORARY EMPLOYEES

Another option to securing workers is to partner with personnel agencies on a contract basis. For long term assignments consider "employee leasing" options. The agency, who is actually considered the worker's employer, will pick up the costs of carrying the worker on their payroll, provide for worker's compensation insurance and in many cases offer benefits to their long-term "employees" (i.e. health insurance, vacation pay). The agency is in business to make a profit so their hourly cost to you for providing their worker in your business facility will be a few dollars more than the worker's actual hourly rate.

The larger your business, the more likely it is that you will need employees to help you in your operation. It is up to you to decide which worker category will be most cost-effective to you. After careful consideration of the matter, you might realize the need for all three categories of workers.

"S" *is for*: SUCCESS

Can you guess the answer to the following question: *What is coveted and sought by many men and women, yet supposedly obtained by only a select percentage of the population?* The answer is **SUCCESS**! *What is success?* Ah, that is the question to which there are many, many answers. Success can be explained as the favorable results or accomplishments of one's attempts and endeavors. Beyond that definition, it is difficult to interpret the true meaning of success as it can mean different things to different people. Success can be as elusive as a butterfly and once attained, it can be as fleeting as a moment.

Why do people seek success? Though there are many reasons why people might seek success, some of the reasons may include: 1) monetary gain, 2) the need to be recognized, 3) the need to be accepted, 4) vanity and/or egotism, 5) the fear of failing and 6) the self satisfaction of knowing one's best efforts have been realized.

Each person's perception of what constitutes success may differ. Some individuals measure success in visual increments: an expensive car, high fashion clothes, acceptance into the "right" social circles, invitations to the "right" places. Some people, by their own standards, may not feel that they have achieved personal success, yet by other's standards these same people may be viewed as very successful. If more emphasis is placed on monetary gain and recognition as measurements of success rather than other factors, then it may explain why some people may not think of themselves as successful. Perhaps success, like beauty, is in the eye of the beholder.

We must not overlook the fact that success can also be measured in portions so small that it can easily be overlooked and not recognized at all. For instance, suppose you have a list of several projects you must complete by the end of the week. You start and complete each project one by one until all the projects have been completed within the specified time frame.

Not only does the completion of all these projects constitute success, but also each individual project accomplishment is also to be considered as achieving success. Often, the "big picture" of long-range goals and objectives may seem so overwhelming that success seems unattainable. In such instances, don't be afraid to break down your goals into smaller segments. Often greater success can be achieved by adhering to the "step-by-step" approach and the "one-day-at-a-time" attitude.

To be successful you must exhibit drive, determination and endurance. Success requires a "stick-to-it" attitude. It is this attitude and the unfaltering belief in one's goals and one's ability to achieve these goals that can make the difference between success and failure.

Successful people are not necessarily smarter than other people are. However, they are probably more focused in their direction and more persistent in their quest for success. Success is there for all that seek it. So go ahead and give it your best shot. Believe you can...Know you can...Show you can... After all, nothing succeeds like *"Success"*!

NOTES:

🗁 CHAPTER 19

EMPLOYEE JOB DESCRIPTIONS & SALARY RANGES

Job Descriptions

Before you can begin to recruit new employees, you must decide on what type of employee you require based on the job description of the work. To establish a job description you will want to write down on paper the total processes involved in your operation. Break down the processes into segments.

Decide how many people it will take to complete each process segment from start to finish. You will want to list the type of worker needed to complete each segment (i.e. assembly worker, secretary, technical support person, engineer, computer analyst, manager etc.) Make note of the skills needed to perform each position, the level of experience this person must possess, the level of completed education necessary to enable him or her to perform this work (entry level, mid-level, senior level). Next write down the exact duties for which this person will be responsible.

Salary Ranges

You must prepare salary ranges for each of your job positions. This information should include beginning salary range, intermediate range and high range for each position.

Resources

Other Businesses - Contact other businesses in your area that offer the same types of products and services as your company. Network with the human resources professionals in these companies and find out if they will share some of their information. Most of the time you will find these people extremely willing to assist you. Surveying three or four like companies in this manner will help you determine your company's salary ranges. You will want to stay as competitive as possible with your wages in order to attract your share of qualified employees. Initially, if your capital will not allow you to meet the same salary standards as your competitors, perhaps you can offer an extra benefit, incentive or perk that will offset the difference.

Benchmark Survey Books - Another way of establishing your salary ranges would be by utilizing benchmark survey books produced to represent specific types of industries (i.e. manufacturing, electronics . . .). Check with your local library to see if this information is available. If not, call upon other human resources professionals in competing businesses. They will probably be able to tell you the purchasing source for this information.

State Employment Department - Your local office of your state's employment development department may also be able to provide you with salary comparisons to other businesses like your own.

Networking - Find out whether or not a networking group exists in your area for human resources professionals. Contact your local office of your state's employment development department and make such an inquiry. These groups provide their members with ongoing updates on labor laws and worker's compensation issues. This powerful networking link to other human resources professionals presents a wonderful opportunity to exchange ideas and discuss matters of mutual concern. The information shared and learned is invaluable and keeps you on the cutting edge of any changes in legislation or laws affecting this important area of your business.

"T" *is for*: TIME MANAGEMENT

There is no time...

Like the present time

To learn how to manage time

In order to save time!

Because most of us wear many hats at work and in our personal lives we can agree that sometimes there is just not enough time in a day to do all the things we have to do. Although we cannot add any more hours to a 24-hour day, we can learn how to utilize our time most efficiently.

There's long been controversy over the use of "lists". Some people like them, others think they are a waste time. Like them or not, with so much to do, one simply cannot rely on one's memory alone. Whether you use a pad of paper, a daily planner book or an electronic organizer, getting organized is the only way to manage your time effectively.

AT WORK - IN YOUR PRESENT POSITION

- Review your schedule in advance for the next day.

- Prioritize your workload.

- Utilize telephone speed-dial/redial buttons.

- Prioritize both your outgoing and incoming mail in the order of their importance.

- Utilize electronic mail (e-mail) to expedite communications.

- If you are conducting a meeting, distribute the meeting agenda in advance so that attendees can be prepared.

- Set a specific meeting start and ending time. Note action items.

- If you are not responsible for setting meetings, but would be involved in attending meeting, you might request that a meeting agenda be distributed in advance.

- Designate someone to take meeting notes during the meeting.

- Distribute meeting notes in a timely manner after the meeting.

- Notify co-workers of your planned absences so they can adjust their workload or work schedule accordingly. You can easily accomplish this using e-mail.

AT HOME

- Plan and/or cook meals in advance.

- Maximize your use of microwave ovens, slow pot cookers etc.

- Shop in bulk at grocery markets and food warehouse stores to save frequency of shopping as well as money and time.

- Incorporate more usable time into your schedule by knowing the business hours (and telephone numbers) of the stores and service companies you frequent. Plan your schedule to take care of as many things as you can in one given area. (For example: If you have to go to the doctor's office and the grocery store and the post office are in close proximity to the doctor, take care of all necessary business in that area and save time.)

THINKING OF STARTING YOUR OWN BUSINESS

- One of the biggest problems that home-based business owners face is being able to separate the familiarity of the home-environment from the newly created business environment. It all comes down to mind-set. If you are thinking of starting your own business, follow the steps in this book as a general guide to keep you focused and help you maximize your output of time.

  Time does not stand still, nor does it wait for anyone. The second hand of a clock will keep ticking off increments of time steadily whether you are organized or not. Make every minute count. You can't add more hours today, but you can use each hour wisely if you just STOP...and think, "POP" (**P**lan ahead / **O**rganize / **P**rioritize)!

📁CHAPTER 20

RECRUITMENT

The key to recruitment is not just filling the employment requisition; it is hiring the candidate whose education, skills and experience level best fit the requirements of the job position. In order to accomplish this most effectively and expeditiously, it is important to understand your company's manpower needs. The job description and salary range of the position will assist you in writing a classified employment advertisement which will outline the basic requirements necessary to attract the very candidates you seek.

<u>Newspaper – Classified Ads</u>

Contact your local newspaper to secure their classified advertising rates. Ad rates are based on word count and length of days the ad will appear in the newspaper as well as the specific days of the week it will appear. Studies indicate that Sunday is the best day of the week to run your ad because more people read the Sunday paper than any other daily newspaper. You may get a better ad rate if your advertisement runs Friday, Saturday and Sunday. Likewise, discounts and contract rates may be offered based on the number of advertisements you place, the length of time your ads appear and the frequency of your company's overall advertising with that particular newspaper.

Display Advertisements

Display ads are priced differently from classified advertisements and are based on the overall size of the ad, layout, format, graphics and other related factors. Display advertising works well for large companies with high dollar advertising budgets, but is usually not a cost-effective option for small business.

Networking

We have discussed networking in Chapter 15 of this book as it relates to procuring new business; however, networking is also a good tool to assist you with your company's recruitment needs. Human Resources networking groups offer ample opportunities for you to make your recruitment needs known to your peers. This network link often provides positive results because job seekers often let their human resources friends and acquaintances know they are looking for new career opportunities. In turn, human resources professionals pass the word on to their peers when such an opportunity presents itself.

Trade Journals and Trade Magazines

These types of publications are a resource for hiring specialized workers such as engineers, electronic technicians, draftsmen, human resources professionals and others. Publications circulation is usually nationwide and as a result small businesses may find the cost of advertising prohibitive. The more specialized the position, the more likely that advertising in these publications will introduce you to the types of candidates your organization is seeking.

State Employment Departments – Local Offices

One responsibility of this state office is to process unemployment insurance claims for people who are no longer employed. Consequently, many state employment offices, like those in California, offer a Job Match program through local state employment development offices. Employers calls their local office and let them know they have a job opening. The employer will give a brief description of the work to be done, the title and salary range of the position, and the education, skill and experience level required perform the work. The office will search their computer system for a "match" of candidates presently on their unemployment roster. If they identify candidates who appear to be a good "fit" for the employer, the state office will contact the employer and set up an employment interview for these candidates. This is an excellent partnership between the public and private sectors and there is no cost to the employer to utilize this service. Contact your local state employment office and find out what types of services and assistance they can offer your company.

I enjoyed an excellent working relationship with my local state employment office when I was in the human resources field in California. On many occasion I was able to avail my employer of the services provided by this excellent resource. Not only did I utilize their Job Match Program, I frequently held interviews on their site when I was looking to recruit a large volume of assembly workers. There was a definite advantage to me in having the opportunity to perform this type of recruitment away from ringing telephones and the possibility of being interrupted by other work-related matters. The collaboration was a successful one for all involved. I filled my employer's recruitment needs and many jobless workers were removed from unemployment rosters, again able to join the ranks of the employed.

Private Industry Councils

State-funded employment programs are often administered by private industry councils in cities throughout the United States. Hiring participants enrolled in designated programs will not only fill your employment openings, but for a specified period of time it may also offer your company a substantial savings on a portion of that employee's wages which would normally be paid by your organization.

Adult Schools/Occupational Centers/Trade Schools

These types of learning institutions usually include, but are not limited to, certification courses in secretarial work, computer skills and engineering. They represent another resource to assist you in finding employees to fit your company's needs.

Colleges

Colleges and Universities represent an excellent source of finding the types of job applicants your company may be seeking. With more and more people of all ages enrolling in college, there is a great likelihood that your efforts will net more than just entry-level candidates.

Job Fairs

Job Fairs are usually organized to represent specific types of individuals (i.e. engineers) of a technical nature. Yet, on occasion you will be able to identify job fairs, which will encompass candidates representing a wider spectrum of industries, fields and skills. Trade journals and trade magazines often carry advertisements of upcoming events, as do neighborhood newspapers. Local offices of state employment offices sometimes organize "reverse-job fairs". In this case, the applicants sit in the 'booths" and the employers stop by to see them, rather than the other way around.

"U" *is for*: UN-

When you first began to read my book you were probably *un*aware of how to turn the concept of business ownership into a tangible means of income for you. *Un*doubtedly you were *un*familiar with many of the aspects that encompass running a successful business operation. Consequently, you were *un*sure as to whether or not being in business for yourself would even be an option you would consider. If you are like most people you resist change and feel somewhat *un*comfortable about facing the *un*known. By the time you reach this page you should have *un*covered enough information for you to determine whether or not self-employment is right for you. So what do you think? Do you have what it takes to be your own boss?

If you remain *un*moved or *un*committed, it may be that you are still *un*convinced. Why? Perhaps, you are still *un*certain as to whether or not you want to assume such a major responsibility. Being your own boss is a <u>BIG</u>

commitment and should not be entered into without serious consideration. Anyone can purchase a business license and open the doors to their establishment. But, there is more to being successful in business than merely opening up your doors for business. You must not be caught *un*prepared. Owning your own business is hard work.

Some people are caught up in the misconception that having a business means working fewer hours, taking off whenever you want and not having to work as hard. These notions are *un*true, especially when your business is in its infancy. Maybe these benefits can be realized over time, but only time will tell . . . As a business owner you will probably work harder and put in longer hours than when you worked for others. The difference is <u>you</u> will set the pace, make the rules, maintain the standards, enjoy the benefits and reap the profits of all your efforts. It is for these very reasons that people opt to get that business license.

But, if you are still *un*decided, I urge you to take your time... Please don't be *un*fair to yourself...it would be *un*bearable to go through life with the feeling of *un*ending guilt because you were *un*willing to put some conscious thought toward how you want to live the rest of your life.

*Un*lock your fears and *un*chain yourself from self-doubt about your career path—present and future.

Self-employment is not for everyone. The important thing is to find out if it is the right thing for you. If it is not, that's okay! At least you will never have to wonder if you *should* have pursued such a direction. If you do discover that you do have what it takes to be your own boss, take a chance on yourself! Self-employment can be a wonderful, fulfilling and _unforgettable_ experience!

NOTES:

🗁CHAPTER 21

THE EMPLOYMENT APPLICATION

I can think of four good reasons (and there's probably more that I haven't thought of) why you should create an employment application for your company.

The **first reason** is for consistency in ensuring that you will be asking each applicant for the same information; the **second reason** is to make it easier to review each applicant and see how he or she compares with the rest of the applicants applying for the same position; the **third reason** is to be able to give written notice to the applicant about your company's employment terms and the **fourth reason** is to have him or her sign an understanding of these terms and give you permission to gather background information.

Make sure you include on the form specific verbiage that indicates such authorization is being asked for and will be binding with the applicant's signature. With regard to the issue of the signature, resumes may be submitted in addition to the job application, but not in lieu of the job application (this information should also be noted on the application). At some future time, should there ever be a question about what was promised or not promised about the position, the fact that you have the applicant's signature on the application will prove to be an advantage to you and your organization. Your application should also explain that applicants must write in all information requested—writing "see resume" is not acceptable. If you live in a "right to work" state, the application should also contain language about "at-will employment" indicating the employee is subject to dismissal or discipline without notice or cause.

"V" *is for*: VISION

The word *vision* implies not only the physical ability to see, but also the mental acuity to look beyond that, which is obvious. Is your range of view near-sighted or far-sighted? Do your eyes see only what is in front of you or are you a person of vision? The resourceful and highly imaginative person of vision need not possess psychic powers or extra sensory perception. Such a person dares only to dream. Yet, the act of dreaming is just the beginning. Floating gently beyond the dream is the vision that enables this individual to actually create and form new ideas which he or she will make...reality.

NOTES:

☐ CHAPTER 22

THE ART OF INTERVIEWING

When we are being interviewed we're filled with anxiety about whether or not we can effectively convince the employer why we are the best candidates for the job. Under the stress of such circumstances, it would be highly unlikely that we'd give any thought at all to the interviewer's point of view regarding the interview itself.

But, interviews *do* take on an entirely different perspective, depending on which side of the desk you sit. If you've never been in the interviewer's seat, there are some things that you should know. It is illegal to discriminate in employment based on:

1)*race* 2)*color* 3)*sex* 4)*religion* 5)*national origin* 6)*disability* 7)*age* 8)*citizenship.* Based on these eight items, be aware that while there is information you can ask for—name, address, work experience, skills, education, employment references, there is information you cannot ask about: age, marital status, dependent information, sexual orientation, health or disability, union affiliation, language ability, personal finances and arrest record. What's more, you must also be careful how you word your questions. Questions that are worded improperly may violate one or more of the discrimination factors previously discussed.

It is important to be consistent in your interviewing techniques. To achieve this, it's a good idea to prepare some written questions (prior to the interview) that are applicable to the job for which you are recruiting. Designate an area at the top of the page for the applicant's name, the date of the interview and the name of the interviewer. If you are operating a small business, you may be conducting all the interviews yourself. If the opportunity allows for others to be part of the interview process, a 3-panel interview is most desirable as it allows for different points of view and ultimately a consensus of opinion to make a final hiring choice. Provide each interviewer with one copy of the questions for each job candidate. Appoint one panel member to explain the interviewing procedure to each applicant. Each panel member would then take a turn asking a question. As each question is asked, the interviewers would document the applicant's answers on their applicant sheet next to the corresponding question.

Some companies conduct only one interview per applicant and then make their final hiring choice. Others opt to review all applicants that have been interviewed and then invite the top three or four candidates back for a second interview based on a different set of questions. Depending on the size and structure of the company, the interviewers in the second interview may or may not be the same individuals who took part in the first interview.

The interview process is designed to help you gather information that will help you to answer the following questions:

1. Is the applicant qualified to do the job?

2. Does the applicant have the educational background, skill level and work history to meet the requirements of the position?

3. Does the applicant reflect the business image consistent with your company's business philosophy?

4. Will the applicant's personality be compatible with the rest of your workforce?

5. Is this applicant the best applicant to fill the open position?

To avoid possible lawsuits involving discrimination or negligent hiring practices, it is highly advisable to learn as much as you can about personnel practices, the employment laws in your state and federal labor laws. In addition to the many good books available on the topics of labor laws, interviewing techniques etc., there are a few nationally recognized companies that offer excellent seminar presentations on a variety of human resources related subjects. Often local human resources groups will sponsor seminars featuring experts in various areas of personnel practices and employment law. Network with employers in your area to identify these groups and find out about the availability of upcoming seminars.

"W" *is for*: WISDOM

Did you ever wonder what makes a wise man (or woman) "wise"? As a child, I often wondered about this very thing. I guess I worried that if I didn't know what made a person wise, then how could I ever hope of one day being wise myself. As a result, I often posed this question in my youth. The answer I received was always the same— *"wisdom"*. But, what exactly *is* wisdom?

If you consult a dictionary, the definition makes reference to wisdom being the quality of being wise. Vague? Yes, I agree. Over the years, the obscurity of such a meaning usually brought me full circle back to the question of: What makes a person wise . . .

I am now considerably older and *wiser* than when I first became concerned about the "wise" and wherefore of life. It is my feeling that wisdom is an intangible quality offering no definitive standard of measurement that can be weighed equally and consistently from one person to the next.

Consequently, any person's opinion, about whom among us are wise and who are considered to be *other*wise, can vary significantly. Just as beauty is in the eyes of the beholder, perhaps wisdom is in the mind of the beholder.

Having made this personal statement of being older and wiser, the sound of my own words echo in my mind, causing me to consciously realize the impact of their profoundness. "Older and wiser": the two words seem to go hand-in-hand. If you are wondering why, I will explain. *If* the quality of wisdom is gained over time, then logically speaking, the older one becomes, the wiser . . .

Knowledge is gained from learning. This process of learning is derived by *living* an event, by personal *participation*, by *observation*, through *reading*, through *research*, through *study* or through *instruction*. On a continual basis, the act of learning provides a greater sense of understanding and awareness of one's self and the world around us.

Knowledge includes the entire range of information the mind has learned, absorbed and stored over the years. Some people are passive about learning and oblivious to the power of knowledge. Other people (like those with an entrepreneurial spirit), quest for knowledge with a strong and all-consuming passion. Motivated by the need to know and the desire to stay informed, this type of individual strives to process information and accumulate knowledge on a daily basis.

One might now wonder that if wisdom is gained from knowledge and knowledge encompasses everything learned in a lifetime, which type of person is the wiser? Ah, but that is not for me to answer and certainly a "wise" person would not dare to say... But, I will say this. I no longer wonder about what makes a wise person wise. For with maturity and age, I have "learned" that with each year lived, another year is added to the total sum of one's knowledge. What is wisdom? My definition would be this: *wisdom* is the cumulative sum of one's life experiences. A wise thought? Let those who are wise be the judge...

NOTES:

🗁 CHAPTER 23

UNDERSTANDING NON-VERBAL
BEHAVIOR
Body Language

Kinetics, the study of bodily movement, is a blending of scientific, social and humanistic study. How a person moves his or her arms and hands, how one walks or stands (posture), or how one gestures with face and/or eyes can tell us a lot about what a person is thinking or feeling at any specific point in time.

Non-verbal communication is sometimes referred to as *body language.* To some degree all of us send and receive non-verbal communication cues on a daily basis—a smile, a wave of the hand, a thumbs up sign, the shaking of hands as a greeting, a yawn of boredom, shaking a fist in anger, clapping hands to show approval . . .

Body language encompasses non-verbal signals that a person voluntarily or involuntarily sends to another. The receiver interprets the behavior as a message based on his or her own perception of the non-verbal messages being sent and sometimes based on a preconception of standardized images processed by the receiver in the form of "stereotypes". What constitutes a stereotype? Stereotypes are "labels" that bias our opinions about certain things or certain groups of people, usually without any basis of fact. For example, our notion that blondes have more fun, that red-heads are hot-tempered, that overweight people are not as intelligent, or share the same feelings as people who are not overweight, that long-styled hair on a woman renders her sexier than her short-haired counterpart.

Factors to consider in non-verbal communication are:

1. Physical Appearance

Hair color, hair style, hair length; height; weight; style of clothing, color of clothing, length of clothing

The way we dress, the styles we wear and the colors we choose tell those around us a lot about whom we are. Though non-verbal, our mode of dress speaks out loudly and clearly to tell and share with the world our views on our personal values our attitudes, our preferences, our goals and our self-esteem. Without consciously realizing its effect, a person's fashion style may influence our interpretation of the non-verbal messages being transmitted.

2. Gestures and Movements

Walking at a slow pace, walking rapidly, taking large strides when walking, taking small steps when walking, shuffling feet when walking; posture: tall and erect vs. slumped over and round-shouldered, gesturing with hands when speaking

3. Face & Eyes

Eye color, eye shape, eye movement; shape of face (round, oval, small chin, large chin), facial expressions; tone of voice, rhythm of voice, inflection of voice

4. Proximity/Space

The distance one stands in proximity to another when they are engaging in general communication

Americans seem to need their "space" in order to feel comfortable when speaking to another person. This feeling of comfort represents approximately one arm's length between the two communicants. If one person **slowly** advances closer, the other person may interpret this non-verbal action as an invasion of his/her space. Though the slow pace of the action may not be cause for alarm, the other person may decide to retreat a few steps backward in order to recapture and maintain his or her former space. The person's facial expression may also change to indicate displeasure over this space invasion. If one person **suddenly** lunges forward, this non-verbal action may cause the other person to react with fright or alarm as he or she instinctively jumps back to reclaim a safe distance between them.

I believe there is a great deal to be learned through observation of human behavior. If I am waiting on line to renew my driver's license at the Department of Motor Vehicles or sitting in the doctor's office waiting till my name is called for my appointment, I utilize the time by watching people in the act of behaving as, and being, themselves. It is fascinating to see how they act or react to different situations, what gestures they make and so forth.

The knowledge I've gained in these instances has proved invaluable to me in interacting with people in both personal and business settings. For example, when I'm conducting an employment interview I consciously observe the applicant's gestures. The head, face and eyes are the most expressive and visual parts of the body. With just a twitch, a grimace, a smile, or a raised eyebrow, the face can exhibit a variety of emotions — confidence, a lack of confidence, confusion, fear, happiness . . .

The non-verbal signals the applicant may be unconsciously sending to me can sometimes be very different from the words they are speaking. I feel I have an acute sense that allows me to decode body movements and decipher unspoken meanings. I've learned to trust my inner instincts. Although I don't claim to be an expert on this subject, I know only that my intuitiveness in this area is something that *works* for me.

Whether you *own* a business and must relate to your customers, clients or employees; or whether you *work* for someone else, the ability to interpret "vibes" and behavioral messages that people voluntarily or involuntarily send to others is definitely an asset that better enables you to effectively communicate with others.

NOTES:

”X” *is for*: “X”

“X” is the 24th letter of the English alphabet. Perhaps the most interesting thing about this letter is that few words begin with it, although many words sound like they do. I was prepared to go the x-*tra* mile to create something x-traordinary that would prove motivational. Unfortunately, I feared it to be an utterly x-*hausting* x-*cercise* in futility. This truth was confirmed as I remained wordless on the subject of “X”; but with one x-*ception...*

I suddenly realized that X” is often used as a reference marker to designate something. Maybe, I could find something motivational about the letter “X” after all. This revelation brought me to a turning point in my thinking that may be x-*plained* with the following visual picture.

Do you see your life as represented in box #1, below?

<u>YOU ARE HERE</u> — (X)

BOX #1:

1. Dissatisfied with present career.
2. Afraid to pursue other employment opportunities.
3. Unsure if self-employment is the answer.
4. Lacks Motivation!
5. Fears the Unknown.
6. Resists change.

If you do, then use the "X" to help you re-x-*amine* your goals. Do you see your life as indicated in box #2, below? There is no x-*cuse* for inaction. You can meet and x-*ceed* your own x-*pectations*.

If you would like to proceed to box #2...

Go ahead and make your mark.

YOU CAN BE HERE — ()

BOX #2:

1. Aware of the opportunities available to you.

2. Empowered to make choices that will affect <u>YOU</u>.

3. Confident to take charge of your own life.

4. Willing and able to make decisions about your career path.

5. Motivated!

6. Ready to make positive changes and face the unknown.

The choice is yours and ✗ marks the spot!

NOTES:

🗀 CHAPTER 24

THE INTERNET CONNECTION

Everyone is talking about the technological innovations born of the Internet, which is often referred to as the *information super highway*. Touted as the best thing that has happened to the world short of the industrial revolution, it is an understatement to say the Internet has revolutionized communications. The Net has brought all points of the globe closer to each other in a manner that allows almost instant access to *any*one, *any*where, in *any* part of the world and at *any*time... How this actually happens is beyond my comprehension from a technical standpoint. I am told this wonder of wonders consists of computers permanently connected from city to city throughout the countries of the world by way of thousands of paths and routes of telephone lines, fiber-optic cables, microwave transmissions and orbiting satellites. No one person actually owns the Internet, but the communication paths made up of these wires and cables and other equipment which comprise the various links *are* owned—usually by instantly recognizable major communication companies. Each individual computer hooked up along this worldwide route makes up a piece of intelligence that becomes part of the overall network system. Computers communicate in a language made up of numeric codes and charts that assign a numeric value to every letter of the alphabet.

Conceived by the United States in the late 1960's, the Internet was initially created by the U.S. Defense Department as a means of exchanging information with military bases, defense contractors, etc. During that time the project was known as DARPANET (Defense Advanced Research Projects Administration). Over time the network evolved to include the exchange of scientific information with other countries throughout the world. The word Defense was dropped and the network was simply referred to as ARPANET.

To take advantage of all that the Internet has to offer, you will need a computer, a modem, a phone line and an on-line service to allow you access to the Internet. America Online, Prodigy, and Compu-Serve are a few of the Internet

Service Providers (ISP) that sell computer access to the Internet.

To access the Web you will have to use a b*rowser.* A Web Browser is a computer program (i.e.: Netscape Navigator, Microsoft Internet Explorer) you load on to your computer that will enable it to retrieve pages of text and graphics from other computers on the Internet, download files, read and post messages and send and receive electronic mail. Embedded in these pages are symbols called *links* that tell your Web Browser where to find other related pages of information on the Internet. When you click on a link it loads another page of text and graphics on to your computer and screen. The idea of following *links* to related pages of information is called *hypertext*.

That brings us to another computer term, *"search engine"...* No, it is not part of a train; it's a piece of software used to conduct a database search of the information you are seeking. There are a number of search engines available to you with some of the more popular ones being:

- Yahoo (http:\\www.yahoo.com);

- Deja News Research Service (http:\\www.dejanews.com);

- Infoseek (http:\\www.guide.infoseek.com);

- Excite (http:\\www.excite.com).

The Internet provides growing access to more than 10,000 topics of information, but just because the information is online does not mean it is authentic or even accurate. You may want to validate Internet information by checking with other sources as well.

When planning your marketing activities, don't overlook the Internet. The Internet offers your company a myriad of opportunities to promote your goods and services—one of which is through the creation of your own business Web Page. When creating your web site, think of it as a "computerized" brochure. Decide what business information you want to make available on your web site. Through *hypertext* your Home Page can link key words and terms to each subsequent page so you will want to carefully design the paths you would like readers to follow when they browse your web.

The Internet has spawned many businesses that specialize in creating web sites. Surf the Web yourself, check the yellow pages, contact your local Chamber of

Commerce or make a phone call to computer stores for more information on how you can identify and contact these professionals. Your local library and neighborhood bookstore also stock a wide selection of books about the Internet and Internet Web Sites—from a scholarly approach geared to "techies" to the step-by-step tutorials.

NOTES:

"Y" *is for*: "YOU"

I've given you to the tools,
but YOU are the craftsman.
I've drawn the blueprint,
but YOU must construct the finished
product to your specifications.
I've prepared the foundation,
but it's up to YOU to build upon it. . .

Rely on the **awareness** I've provided. Stick to your **beliefs**, but remember **change** can be positive. Call upon your **determination** to give you strength as you look to **empowerment** to energize you. Live your **future** — today!

Set **goals** and let go of bad **habits**. Don't forget that it's a good **idea** to keep a **journal**. The **knowledge** you derive from it will be invaluable to you, no matter what course of action you follow. Be the **leader** of your own life. Give yourself permission to succeed. Draw upon your skills and talents and you **may** just find your own special **niche**.

Good **organization** is important in all you do. This is just one of many administrative skills that will help you achieve whatever success you seek. Use **perception** to your advantage and create your own reality. Set high standards and keep in mind that **quality** does count!

Take advantage of all **resources** available to you. You have the power to make your own **success**. Incorporate **time management** techniques into your daily routine and maximize your productivity. **Un**derstand no one can do it for you. It's all up to you!

Be a person of **vision** and look beyond all that is around you. The **wisdom** you gain will last you a lifetime. . . You are here now. Decide where you want to be and how you will get there— "**X**" marks the spot!

That brings us to "Y"...and "Y" is for **you**. It's always been about you. Hopefully you now realize that you are the keeper of your own destiny and everything you do depends on you. It doesn't matter who you work for as long as you take charge of your own life... So go for it! Take that one all-important step. Walk; no LEAP, into the first day of the rest of your life. If you ask "Y", it's because "Y" is for **YOU**!

🗁CHAPTER 25

COMING TO…TERMS

This chapter is dedicated to terms that you may want to reference. I've compiled this information for easy access and categorized it for your convenience.

BASIC INTERNET TERMS

ASCII – American Standard Code for Information Interchange. This is a text format readable by all computers.

Attachment – a file included with e-mail.

E-MAIL – electronic mail.

HTML – Hypertext Markup Language. The language used to create web documents.

HTTP – Hypertext Transfer Protocol – The language command used to transfer text from computer to computer via the Internet.

IAP – Internet Access Provider is a company that charges a fee and sell connection to the Internet.

URL – Uniform Resource Locator (the addressing system for the World Wide Web).

WWW – World Wide Web.

BUSINESS FINANCIAL TERMS

Accrued Liabilities – an accumulation of anything owed (wages, earned commissions, interest on loans, taxes).

Assets – anything of value owned by a company or individual.

Balance Sheet – a statement showing assets, liabilities and net worth as of specific date.

Cost of Goods Sold – beginning inventory plus purchases, less ending inventory.

Financial Statement – Balance sheet and Profit and Loss Statement.

Gross Profit – gross income less cost of goods sold.

Liabilities – anything owed.

Net Worth – anything of value owned by a company or individual after liabilities are subtracted from the assets.

Profit and Loss Statement – a statement showing gross income, expenses of operation and net profit (or loss) for a specific period of time.

Recurring Expenses – monies that must be paid out continually on a monthly, quarterly or annual basis (rent, utility bills, insurance premiums).

BUSINESS OWNERSHIP TERMS

Business Opportunity – involves the sale of personal (chattel), rather than real, property. Such a sale includes inventory, fixtures, goodwill and the assignment of a license or lease.

Contract – an agreement between two or more people setting forth the specific terms of the obligation. Real estate contracts must be in writing.

Corporation – consisting of a group of persons, a corporation is established and treated as an individual with rights and liabilities distinct and apart from those of the persons involved therein. A corporation has certain powers and duties of a natural person and under state corporation laws, a corporation may continue to exist for any length of time as prescribed by law.

DBA – Doing Business As (refers to the name you choose for your business).

Fictitious Firm Name – the name of your business.

Fixtures – trade fixtures are items of equipment that are specific to a particular business or trade (i.e. kitchen equipment in a restaurant, coffee beverage making machines in a specialty coffee shop).

Franchise – permission given from a manufacturer or corporation owner to a distributor or retailer which gives entitlement to that distributor or retailer to sell the owner's products.

Franchisee – Distributor or retailer entitled to sell an owner's products.

Franchiser – manufacturer or corporation owner who gives entitlement to others to sell the owner's products.

Goodwill – represents the expectation of continued patronage of the business's current customer base.

Inventory – stock being transferred.

Lease – is a contract between a lessor and a lessee setting forth consideration, a specified term for which the lessee may occupy the real property, as well as the conditions relating to the tenant's use of the designated property.

Leasehold – another term for lease.

Lease Interest – another term for lease.

Lessee – person who leases the property (tenant).

Lessor – person who owns the property and is causing it to be leased (landlord).

Partnership – voluntary association between two or more persons to participate in a business or venture under specific terms which are defined and mutually agreed upon as to participation, profit and losses.

Rent – monetary consideration specified to be paid per the conditions of a lease.

Retail – the sale of small quantity goods direct to the consumer.

Sole Proprietor – exclusive ownership of a business by only one individual.

Wholesale – the purchase of goods in large quantities by a retailer from a distributor or manufacturer for resale to the consumer.

BUSINESS TERMS

Consumer – one who buys goods or services for personal use.

Customer – one who buys goods or services for personal use.

Mini-Mall – small cluster of businesses built on one piece of property.

Industrial Park – a planned area designed for industrial use.

Landlord – person who owns the property being rented.

Strip-Mall – another name for a mini-mall.

Store – a retail establishment where goods are offered for sale to the consumer.

Storefront – a unit of space on the ground floor of a building designed for use as a retail store.

Tenant – person who pays rent to occupy space (i.e. in a building, office or storefront).

"Z" *is for*: ZING, ZIP AND ZEST

Put

a little

zing

in your life

and lots of

zip

in your pace.

Life is what you make of it,

So take an active part in the race.

You can be whatever you choose,

If you are willing to put yourself to the test.

Life is what you make of it...

Live it with

zing,

Live it with

zip,

Live it with

zest!

ABOUT THE AUTHOR

Jo Ann M. Colton is a published writer and entrepreneur. Her professional work history includes employment in local government, as well as diverse private sector positions in the fields of aerospace, building and construction, computer peripherals manufacturing, and research and development. Her employment skills and knowledge have been realized in the areas of public affairs, customer relations, administration, marketing, supervision and management, human resources management and human resources consulting. In addition, Ms. Colton was a licensed California realtor for 12 years.

Jo Ann M. Colton also has first-hand experience as both a sole proprietor and business partner in business ventures that have included: independent liquor and grocery markets, women's apparel retail sales (fashion shows and personal clothes shopping for women) and two promotional business/personal writing services.

www.ingramcontent.com/pod-product-compliance
Lightning Source LLC
Chambersburg PA
CBHW030428290526
45786CB00001B/191